BECOMING THE EDUCATOR
THEY NEED

ROBERT JACKSON

FOREWORD BY PEDRO NOGUERA

Strategies, Mindsets, and Beliefs
for Supporting Male Black
and Latino Students

BECOMING THE EDUCATOR
THEY NEED

ascd   Alexandria, Virginia USA

2800 Shirlington Road, Suite 1001 • Arlington, VA 22206 USA
Phone: 800-933-2723 or 703-578-9600 • Fax: 703-575-5400
Website: www.ascd.org • E-mail: member@ascd.org
Author guidelines: www.ascd.org/write

Ronn Nozoe, *Interim CEO and Executive Director;* Stefani Roth, *Publisher;* Genny Ostertag, *Director, Content Acquisitions;* Allison Scott, *Acquisitions Editor;* Julie Houtz, *Director, Book Editing & Production;* Joy Scott Ressler, *Editor;* Judi Connelly, *Senior Art Director;* Mary Duran, *Graphic Designer;* Keith Demmons, *Production Designer;* Kelly Marshall, *Interim Manager, Production Services;* Trinay Blake, *E-Publishing Specialist.*

PAPERBACK ISBN: 978-1-4166-2820-0   ASCD product #119010   n8/19
PDF E-BOOK ISBN: 978-1-4166-2822-4; see Books in Print for other formats.

Quantity discounts are available: e-mail programteam@ascd.org or call 800-933-2723, ext. 5773, or 703-575-5773. For desk copies, go to www.ascd.org/deskcopy.

Library of Congress Cataloging-in-Publication Data
Names: Jackson, Robert (Educator) author.
Title: Becoming the educator they need: strategies, mindsets, and beliefs
   for supporting male black and Latino students / Robert Jackson.
Description: Alexandria, VA: ASCD, [2019] | Includes bibliographical
   references and index.
Identifiers: LCCN 2019009812 (print) | LCCN 2019981453 (ebook) | ISBN
   9781416628200 (paperback) | ISBN 9781416628224 (pdf)
Subjects: LCSH: African American boys--Education. | Hispanic American
   teenage boys--Education. | Teacher effectiveness. | Multicultural
   education. | Mentoring in education. | Teacher-student relationships.
Classification: LCC LC2731.J32 2019 (print) | LCC LC2731 (ebook) | DDC
   371.829/96073--dc23
LC record available at https://lccn.loc.gov/2019009812
LC ebook record available at https://lccn.loc.gov/2019981453

30 29 28 27 26 25 24 23 22   6 7 8 9 10 11 12

BECOMING THE EDUCATOR
THEY NEED

FOREWORD

In America, Black and Latino males are overrepresented in categories typically associated with hardship and defeat. They experience disproportionately high rates of unemployment, incarceration, and homicide, and many of them are so disenfranchised (approximately 34 percent of Black males between the ages of 16 and 34) that they are literally "missing" from key census data because they are neither working, in school or college, or in the criminal justice system (Patterson, 2015).

In most schools and districts throughout the United States, Black, and in many cases Latino, males are overrepresented in educational categories typically associated with failure and subpar academic performance—dropout and suspension rates, special education placements, and college readiness programs. However, on indicators associated with success—enrollment in honors, gifted classes, and advanced placement courses, matriculation to college, and degree attainment—Black and Latino males tend to be vastly underrepresented. With few exceptions, these dismal patterns are evident in urban, suburban, and rural school districts throughout the United States—even in communities with relatively small minority populations.

These patterns are pervasive throughout the United States, and they have been in place for many years. Rather than urgency, there is a profound and disturbing sense of resignation about our ability as a nation to counter these dismal trends.

Becoming the Educator They Need provides clear and practical guidance to educators and others on what can be done to support boys and young men of color. Drawing upon his life experience and his work as an educator and advisor to schools throughout the country, Jackson outlines strategies and practices that can be helpful in countering the negative trends and altering the life trajectories of young Black and Latino males.

For those in search of solutions and who seek to make a difference in the lives of young men, this book will be an insightful resource.

Pedro Noguera
August 2019

INTRODUCTION

When I was 16 years old, my best friend, Tony Binion, was murdered. I remember how he laid there while people stood around staring intently at his body (which, at the insistence of the police, remained uncovered so as not to disturb the crime scene). I remember people, including family members and close friends, screaming and crying. We were so young. Neither of us had even begun to grow facial hair. Prior to the incident, Tony was at a party from which another young man, who was being disruptive, had been thrown out. After a time, the young man returned and began randomly shooting into a crowd of people, among them Tony and a few of his friends. As people scattered, Tony was shot in the chest and died at the scene.

The next morning, the headline on the front page of the newspaper read, "Shooting Victim, Good Kid," and a photo of Tony accompanied the article. I was sick to my stomach. Tears rolled down my face. The hurt I felt that day and after was excruciating. It seemed as though the rest of the world was able to move on, but my life stopped for a moment that day. This was not how Tony's and my story was supposed to end. Tony and I were going to be roommates in college, each other's best man at our weddings, and godfathers to each other's children. We had dreams of going to the pros—Tony to the NBA and me to the NFL. Like too many other young Black and Latino males, Tony's life was cut short before it could truly begin.

When I returned to school on the Tuesday following Tony's funeral, one of my teachers said something that fueled both my anger and my will to prove her wrong. She said that I was wasting my time [by coming back to school] because kids from my community didn't succeed in life. Her comment made it clear to me that she found no fulfillment in educating me. Her perception had become her reality. She was convinced that her implicit biases about young Latino males and young men who looked like me were right. I checked out of her class mentally for the remainder of that semester because I knew she didn't want me to succeed. I knew that she was just there to, as she would often state, "pass the time and get her paycheck."

When students know you don't care if they succeed, it's tough for them to focus and push themselves. I knew my teacher had her mind made up about the Black and Latino males in my class. When she interacted with us, she was distant, and when she spoke to us, it was only to scold us or make sarcastic comments. She didn't even try to hide her true feelings. I knew her perceptions of me were wrong, but as a 16-year-old with low self-esteem who was living in poverty, socially and economically disadvantaged, and living in a stressful situation at home in a violent neighborhood, I wondered if her opinion of me was right. However, regardless of her opinion of me, I wanted to be successful.

Fortunately, I also had teachers who supported and inspired me while growing up. The one I recall most fondly is my elementary teacher—Dr. Delores Sangster.

Mrs. Sangster exemplified discipline and accountability. She set high expectations for all her students, and my classmates and I understood that she expected us to do well. When we heard her heels clicking up the hallway, we immediately began to assess our behavior and adjust it accordingly. All talking ceased, and we would find our seats and sit at attention. Mrs. Sangster wasn't the one who you wanted to upset or disappoint by breaking the rules; there were consequences for that, and my classmates and I tried to avoid them at all cost.

One of my classmates, Glenn Dillard, and I just didn't get along with each other. We fought often, and Mrs. Sangster would take us into a small room and give us each three whacks with the paddle. (Mrs. Sangster's discipline was tougher than some of the hits that I took as a football player for 20 years). After she paddled me, she would always sit me down to talk. Though, with my bottom stinging, I had to struggle to focus and remain attentive; it was worth the effort because Mrs. Sangster would tell me how great I was and how much potential I had to be greater in life. She told me I was a success story waiting to happen. She saw the value in the fact that I loved to talk and told me that one day I would be speaking in front of thousands of people. Guess what? That's exactly what I do for a living today. Mrs. Sangster "spoke me" here.

Educators must use their words wisely because words affect students both positively and negatively. When students are coming from tough circumstances, a positive word can give them hope. Some of the young men in your class are extremely broken and need a positive voice.

―――――――

When I was in elementary school, I was extremely hurt on most days. My stepfather, who had been physically, verbally, and mentally abusive, would walk around our house for weeks and not say two words to me. But Mrs. Sangster both spoke to me and saw something in me. I didn't know or have a relationship with my biological father, whom I strongly resemble. Even though I at times didn't like who I was or know who I was, Mrs. Sangster called me a king—and meant it. She said it so often that one day I started to believe it. One day, a young man "called me out of my name,"* and I told him, "I don't care what you call me. Mrs. Sangster said I was a king." Her words resonated with me. She spoke positive words to me and my classmates every day; some of us received them and some of us dismissed them.

About nine years ago, I delivered a keynote address at a large educational conference. As I sat on the stage waiting to be introduced, I glanced to my left, and guess who I saw in the front row?—Mrs. Sangster! I was so excited that, after being introduced, I momentarily forgot that I was there to give a keynote address, and the first thing I said was, "Hey, there is Mrs. Sangster, my former teacher!" I explained to the audience who Mrs. Sangster was and the influence she had on my life as a student at a young age and how she was that one caring adult who I needed at that time. The audience gave her a standing ovation. Tears rolled down her cheeks. She yelled out, "I knew you could do it! I knew you could do it!" I jumped off the stage and down into the audience to give her a hug. I was thankful I didn't hurt myself (the long jump from the stage to the floor was fueled by adrenaline and excitement). As I approached her to hug her and give her a kiss on the cheek,

*Referring to someone in an insulting way.

she whispered in my ear as the crowd looked on, "You and your classmates were some bad kids!"

Mrs. Sangster's remark made me chuckle because she never told my classmates and me as children that we were bad; she waited until I was the man she knew I could become. She understood that, as a child, I was going through enough trauma and that fire is not put out with more fire. Other teachers referred to us every day in negative terms—at risk, bad kids, not smart, special ed students (implying that all of us had learning disabilities), not intelligent, a menace to society, not college material, hopeless, criminals, mistakes, cursed people, less than, and so on. Because of Mrs. Sangster's positive words and the frequency with which I heard them, I felt empowered to be whatever I set my mind to be. Unlike many other teachers, Mrs. Sangster tried to uplift my classmates and me with her words—and she brought out the best in us. She found fulfillment in educating *all* her students. Her words positively affirmed me and my male classmates of color.

A few years ago, Mrs. Sangster, after spending more than 45 years in education, succumbed to cancer. She left behind a legacy of giving her students the option to get it right. Outside the church where the service was held, there was a line around the corner of people waiting to pay their respects, and the church was filled beyond capacity. During the service, former students shared their experiences with Mrs. Sangster, telling of how she influenced their lives and made them who they were as adults. I was asked by her family to deliver a message at the funeral, which was an honor as she had so many students from which they could have chosen. (I found out later that Mrs. Sangster had followed me through high school and college and throughout my professional career, and that she would tell her colleagues, "Robert Jackson was one of my babies.") Although I had other teachers through the years, Mrs. Sangster was the one teacher who claimed me as hers—and I'll never forget that.

How often do you tell your Black and Latino male students that, despite their circumstances or their backgrounds, they will be success stories? How often do you affirm these young men? How often do you appoint them as leaders in your building? How many of them know that their lives *do* matter and that what is said about them in the media isn't necessarily true? How many of them do you call your "babies" or your "kids?" Speaking positive affirmations to students every day can truly help you build relationships with students and help educators and administrators connect with these young men.

If all successful people were honest with themselves, they would be able to think back to that one caring adult or mentor who took the time to help them discover their potential, help them know that it's OK to dream about their future, and understand that it is OK to make bad decisions and how to bounce back from adversity. They wouldn't be able to share the story of their lives without remembering that one vital, unforgettable person —their Mrs. Sangster—who taught them how to be better versions of themselves and was relentless about their success.

My hope is that this book will show you how to be that vital, unforgettable person for your Black and Latino male students—the most underserved, suspended, and expelled students in education. They are also the most likely to be incarcerated, drop out of school, and become victims of homicide—like my friend Tony Binion. Students will not always remember what you taught them, but they will always remember how you made them feel. When former students contact me or come back to see me, it's always about the life lessons I taught them and how they are using them, not about the subject I taught them.

What will your students say when they come back to see you?

CHAPTER 1

Cultural Awareness:
Understanding the Realities of
Life for Black and Latino Males

We live in a world where many young Black and Latino males gravitate toward gangs because the gang members treat them more like family than their own parents do. According to the National Gang Center, in 2011, 46.2 percent of gang members were Hispanic or Latino and 35.3 percent were Black (as compared to only 11.5 percent white and 7 percent classified as "other") (2018). A disproportionate number of Black and Latino youth also live in poverty: in 2017, roughly 33 percent of Black youth and 26 percent of Latino youth lived in families with incomes below the federal poverty level (Anne E. Casey Foundation). When students living in poverty are arrested and booked (often unfairly), bonds can be set as high as $3,000 to $5,000—which they can't afford to pay. One in three Black males and one in six Latino males born in or after the year 2001 will spend time in prison at some point in his life (The Sentencing Project, 2017), a status quo that the private prison system does much to exacerbate. Private prisons in the United States make an annual profit of more than $3.3 billion for incarcerating individuals (Cohen, 2015)—most of whom have black and brown faces, and many of whom have committed minor offenses. Even more disturbing is the fact that Black and Latino males are also disproportionately at risk of being murdered. According to the Centers for Disease Control and Prevention, homicide is the leading cause of death for Black males ages 15 to 24 (2018a) and the second leading cause of death for Hispanic males ages 15 to 34 (2018b). These numbers are disturbing.

The following account is illustrative of the plight of many Black male youths.

Kalief Browder

In 2010, 16-year-old Kalief Browder of the Bronx, New York, was accused of stealing a backpack, the contents of which included $700, a credit card, and a laptop. When he and his friends were stopped by the police, although he stated that he hadn't stolen the backpack, the police insisted that he had. After he was thoroughly searched by the police, who did not find the backpack or any of its contents on him, he was arrested.

After being unjustly arrested, Browder was told that if he pleaded guilty, he would be charged for stealing the backpack and allowed to go home. He refused to "deal," as he'd stated that he hadn't committed the crime and didn't want a blemish, particularly one that was unwarranted, on his record to jeopardize his plan to attend college on a wrestling scholarship.

He was imprisoned, and his bond was set at $3,500. As neither he nor his family had the money to get him out of jail on bond, he spent three years in Riker's Island, one of the toughest prisons in the United States, awaiting a trial date that was never set. While at Riker's, he endured starvation and physical and sexual assaults from guards and prisoners. Of the more than 1,000 days that he spent at Riker's, 800 or more were spent in solitary confinement.

After three years, someone powerful heard about his case, spoke out against it, and Browder was released from prison. However, by that time, he had missed sitting for the SATs, his high school graduation and prom, and the opportunity to attend college on a scholarship. After his release, he experienced nightmares and depression and every day feared returning to prison. Mentally, he couldn't cope and attempted suicide on more than one occasion. Even though someone who'd heard about his story paid for him to go to community college, his struggles with anxiety and depression worsened.

Two years after being released from prison for a crime he didn't commit, Kalief Browder died after hanging himself outside his parents' home. He was only 22 years old. Sixteen months after Kalief committed suicide, his mother died of a heart attack (though many say she died of a broken heart).

This is one of many tragic stories of young men of color that educators never hear about. Kalief's life mattered. His mother's life mattered.

Factors That Specifically Affect Male Youths of Color

The statistics mentioned previously are due to a vast array of factors affecting black and brown young men, the most insidious of which are deeply rooted in our culture and present structural barriers to success in school and in life. Here we discuss five of these factors:

- Invisibilization
- Marginalization
- Pre-criminalization
- Stereotype threat
- Colorism

Invisibilization

Cases in point. Invisibilization is the act of seeing a person or situation as invisible, as not important, and without breadth or depth. Think of how the public at large reacts to the police killing of an unarmed Black or Latino man as compared to a dog being mistreated (Michael Vick served more than two years in prison for his participation in a dog-fighting ring that led to the deaths of several dogs). Black men are murdered for minor offenses every day.

LaQuan McDonald

On October 20, 2014, 17-year-old LaQuan McDonald was shot 16 times by police officer Jason Van Dyke as he, with a small knife in his hand, was walking away from Van Dyke. Van Dyke and his fellow officers tried to cover up the crime and stated that McDonald "came at" Van Dyke, but a video showed a totally different story. After more than four years, Van Dyke was found guilty of second-degree murder and aggravated battery and sentenced to seven years in prison.

Note that, with good behavior, Van Dyke could be released from prison in a little over two years—the length of time that Michael Vick spent in jail for his part in the dog-fighting ring. Then there is the case of Michael Brown.

Michael Brown

On August 9, 2014, shortly after his 18th birthday and high school graduation, Michael Brown was fatally shot by 28-year-old white police officer Darren Wilson in Ferguson, Missouri. An altercation took place, and Michael Brown and his friend were pursued by Officer Wilson. In the end, although Brown was unarmed, 12 shots were fired at him—and among the six that hit him was the fatal shot to his head. Brown died at the scene. His body lay uncovered for several hours while people from the neighborhood, including children, passed by before finally being covered. Wilson was acquitted of all charges and reassigned to another city and continues to serve as a police officer.

As this story, which was on every news station in the United States and many abroad, shows, when police officers shoot an unarmed Black or Latino male, they generally get off with a slap on the wrist while a family is tormented by the death of their loved one.

White men who commit atrocities are taken into custody unharmed.

Dylan Roof

Dylan Roof was a white supremacist who, at the age of 21, on July 17, 2015, walked into Emanuel African Methodist Episcopal Church in Charleston, South Carolina, and murdered nine innocent people. Among those murdered were the senior pastor of the church and a state senator. Roof was identified by those who survived the shooting. A manhunt ensued, and Roof was apprehended without so much as a scratch on him. (In fact, police granted his request to stop by Burger King on his way to jail because he was hungry.) He later confessed to the shootings—stating that he hoped to ignite a race war by killing innocent people at a church—and stated that his views came from the 2012 shooting death of Trayvon Martin. On December 15, 2016, he was convicted in federal court of 33 charges, including hate crimes. He was sentenced to life in prison without the possibility of parole.

That one (Black) young man hurt no one and was murdered and one (white) young man killed nine people and was not harmed at all perfectly exemplifies invisibilization—that is, if it's not happening in your world, it's of no importance to you.

In the classroom. Invisibilization occurs in the classroom when some teachers and administrators take the word of white students over that of Black or Latino male students—even when the former are at fault for harassing the latter.

I attended a mostly white suburban school in which 96 percent of the students were white and 4 percent were Black, Asian, and Indian. I was one of five Black students on the football team. During my senior year, I was attacked by a white student. Everyone knew I was a star athlete with good grades on my way to a Division 1 college or university to play football and run track. Even though I was physically assaulted by a white student, I was the one put in handcuffs by the police officer called to the scene while the white student was treated as the victim. As I was sitting on the floor, unjustly handcuffed, the white student ran over and kicked me. While still in handcuffs, I hopped to my feet and was immediately grabbed by police officers and school administrators aggressively and yelled at like I was the perpetrator. Again, no one ever addressed the fact that the white student had assaulted me—twice. The white student was never disciplined. He was sent back to class. He laughed at me as he walked away. I was placed on in-school suspension—stuck in a small room staring at the wall all day. I felt like I was in a prison cell.

As the MVP of the football team, that incident almost cost me my scholarship to college. The day after two prominent community leaders came to my school to discuss the injustice and threatened to call the news stations, I was allowed to return to my classroom, and the incident was never mentioned again. The scars remained, and they ran deep. I never forgot that incident and how powerless I felt. The people who were supposed to protect me—the teachers and administrators—didn't.

This is how our young men of color are prepared for prison. I felt like my life didn't matter; like no matter what happened to me, the people with power weren't on my side. This is how many of your Black and Latino male students feel, and they act out as a result of it. I have personally heard some of their stories.

Marginalization

Marginalization is when someone is relegated to a powerless or unimportant position within a society or group due to a given characteristic like race or ethnicity. This occurs in the housing market, workforce, legal system, and educational system. When two students of different races commit the same offense at the same age and receive different punishment, that's marginalization. When two students of different races do equally well in something and one receives recognition and the other somehow gets second best, that's marginalization.

I became fully aware of the effects of marginalization when I was bussed to an all-white suburban school back in the mid-1980s while entering the 5th grade. I knew right away this school was different.

Police cars and dogs were everywhere as I entered the school building for the first time. At my old public school, I had friends of all colors, and we never discussed race or treated each other differently. At this particular school, it was obvious from day one that the color of one's skin mattered. I remember being put in a room with other Black students from my neighborhood. (It turns out we were all considered remedial students, even though we hadn't showed any indication that we were remedial students.) We were told that we had to take a series of exams in order to be placed in regular classes with our new classmates. The way they explained it was very condescending and made many of us feel uncomfortable and inferior. In fact, some of my Black classmates accepted the inferior status that was put on us and acted out until they were kicked out of school. We were told that we weren't smart enough to be in classes with our new white classmates.

I had a chip on my shoulder and wanted to prove them all wrong. I focused with everything I had and passed the tests that I was given. I knew I was smart. Although I was moved to a general education classroom, I was at times treated like I shouldn't be there. I was almost always the only student of color in my classes. Teachers made patronizing comments toward me. A teacher once said to me, "Just get out!" because I didn't know the answer to a question. (I knew the answer but was nervous and unsure.) Being the only student of color in my classes often made me feel inferior. I got tired of the racist jokes and inappropriate comments made by my classmates. I didn't have the latest brands in clothing or shoes. Life was tough enough without extra pressure from my peers.

If you call someone dumb long enough and treat them as though they are not smart, they will start believing you and will act the part. If you continue to question someone's intellectual abilities, it will start affecting them mentally—especially younger students whose minds are not fully developed. I was very nervous while taking exams because I knew I wasn't expected to pass. I, as do many of Black and Latino kids I work with daily, felt like my teachers expected me to fail. I knew that most of my teachers, coaches, and administrators didn't believe in me. Many of the young men today have been beaten down so much by life that they have given up. When educators give up on them, they give up on themselves. When we took tests, teachers walked up and down the rows watching, displaying zero empathy. Most of the kids were intimidated and stopped trying. A student who sat close to me said, "They think we are all dumb anyway. We might as well prove them right. I'm going to just mark anything for the answers."

I could tell on my first day at school that kids of color were going to be marginalized. The atmosphere was toxic. Everyone was uncomfortable, including the students who were bussed in, the students who had been there, and the educators, who had a hard time hiding just how extremely uncomfortable they were with having to work with students who looked like me.

During one class, still during the first week of school, a classmate's father burst open the door, rushed in to the classroom, and snatched his daughter, saying, "My daughter is not going to school with raccoons and possums." (Shortly before he had rushed in, his daughter asked me my name and shook my hand. She told me her name was Sarah. She didn't see race as an issue. She tried to get to know me.)

Sarah's father jerked her out of her chair and hauled her out of the classroom. I never saw Sarah again.

Sarah's father was teaching Sarah at a young age to stay away from people who did not look like her. Her biases were being formed by her father's responses. She was learning early in life to think of students of color as "less than" and to stay away from them.

———

I said to my mother that night, "I'm not going back to that school. They have raccoons and possums in there." My mother's eyes widened and her jaw dropped. There was a troubling look behind her eyes. Although she was clearly very angry, she didn't say anything to me about it. She addressed the matter at the school. Once I understood that Sarah's father was referring to me and the other Black students from my neighborhood as raccoons and possums, I understood why my mother was angry. (My mother had been raised in the Deep South [Mississippi] in the 1950s and 1960s and, as a little girl, saw racism first-hand. She saw "Whites Only" and "Colored Only" signs on restroom doors, above water fountains, and in restaurants. She never thought her son would have to experience racism—especially since she'd moved from the prejudiced South to the Midwest.)

My 5th grade experience has stayed with me all these years. I saw how that first day at school affected the lives of my classmates in a negative way and changed the trajectory of their lives. It's our job as educators to help students change the narrative and their perspectives and be accepting of everyone —regardless of race.

Pre-criminalization

This is the tendency to perceive Black and Latino males as criminals when they haven't done anything wrong. If society and educators continue to look at students as if they are criminals, they will unconsciously treat them as such. When a white kid gets in trouble, society makes excuses, saying things such as, "Oh, he is just acting out because his parents got a divorce." The reality is that a very small percentage of Black and Latino kids are criminals. Most are success stories in the making, and that's how we should treat them. They, as do their white counterparts, have issues at home (such as divorced parents) and at school. Also, two kids from the same household, block, or neighborhood may present very differently. Society can't continue to group all kids from a neighborhood or race as one particular type.

One of the best-known and most glaring examples of pre-criminalization is the fact that young males of color are pulled over while driving at far higher rates in this country than are males of any other race. Black drivers are 20 percent more likely to be pulled over in traffic stops than are white drivers, and Hispanic drivers are 30 percent more likely than whites to be pulled over (Stanford Open Policing Project, 2018). An alarming number of the young men of color pulled over are then treated as criminals, and too many have been arrested, shot, or killed—even in instances where no criminal activity had taken place. How is it that so many young men of color don't walk away from what are supposed to be routine traffic stops? How is it that so many students of color are being treated as criminals because they may have a parent in jail or family members who are criminals?

On July 6, 2016, Philando Castile, who knew the first and last names of all the students at the school where he worked, was a victim of pre-criminalization.

Philando Castile

Philando Castile, a 32-year-old Black male, was shot seven times by police officer Jeronimo Yanez after being pulled over while driving in Falcon Heights, Minnesota. Prior to the incident, Castile, who had no criminal record and who had been driving with his girlfriend and her four-year-old daughter, was reaching for his license and registration, which officer Yanez requested. Yanez claimed that he thought Castile was reaching for his registered firearm. Castile died within a half hour of having sustained the gunshot wounds. Officer Yanez, charged with three felonies, was acquitted of all charges.

Black and Latino males of all ages are treated like criminals despite not having displayed any type of criminal behavior or being involved in any criminal activity. Many people have their minds made up about Black and Latino males whose physical description is similar to Castile's (who wore dreadlocks). The fact that he was an upstanding citizen meant nothing because, in the minds of many, his appearance was that of a criminal.

Early pre-criminalization occurs every day in our schools. When some educators take one look at some young men of color, they judge them based on the fact that they look like what they perceive offenders look like. Early pre-criminalization occurs when teachers perceive a student who is not actively participating as being disrespectful. Consider the fact that a student may be shy, timid, uncomfortable with the way he sounds, or attempting to grasp the information before putting himself out there or before jumping to (often unfounded) conclusions.

Stereotype Threat

This refers to the fear of affirming a negative stereotype associated with one's race, gender, ethnicity, or cultural group. According to psychologists Claude Steele, Joshua Aronson, and Steven Spencer, stereotype threat causes anxiety in students during tests and therefore plays a significant part in widening the achievement gap. Their work shows that when people experience even subtle reminders that they belong to a group believed to be inferior academically, it has a negative effect on them (American Psychological Association, 2006).

Black and Latino kids hear what is said about them on the news. When race is brought up on exams or anywhere else, they may shut down or wonder if they will be treated fairly or if their race will play a role in the test results. It's hard for students under stress or duress to perform well on exams. Educators can assist their students by gaining a better understanding of and paying closer attention to the psychological processes of stereotyped threats. If there are subtle hints of race inferiority in your school system, call attention to them and take steps to remove them.

Colorism

Colorism is prejudice or discrimination within an ethnic group against individuals with darker complexions. For Black Americans, this began during slavery (during which time Blacks with lighter complexions were given the opportunity to work in the house, while those with darker complexions were forced to work in the fields, resulting in a division within the race). This phenomenon is common within ethnic groups in places where Europeans imposed racial hierarchies featuring themselves at the top (e.g., India, Australia, the Caribbean, Latin America).

Colorism still causes divisions—whether regarding self-esteem, self-image, self-discipline, self-actualization, or self-control. It is also perpetuated by the fashion industry's idea of what is beautiful and acceptable and what isn't. Educators may sometimes judge and stereotype students based on the depth of pigmentation in their skin tone. We should never belittle another human being because of race or color tone. We have to appreciate one another for each of our unique differences. If this is something you have been taught, it must be erased from your existence if you would like these young men to have a fair chance to succeed.

Linguistic and Religious Diversity

According to the National Center for Education Statistics, English language learners constituted an average of 14 percent of total public-school enrollment in cities, 9.1 percent in suburban areas, 6.5 percent in towns, and 3.6 percent in rural areas (2018). Many of your students' parents may not have been born in the United States, so communication may be difficult. Some parents are easily irritated and uncomfortable because they don't know the language. Getting frustrated with the communication gap isn't going to help you, your students, or their parents. Schools must have Spanish-speaking (and other necessary language) resources and interpreters for students and their parents.

While I was speaking to parents in a school district in California, one father stated that he was very upset by the fact that his daughter intentionally spoke English at home when he didn't allow English to be spoken in the home because she was the only one who spoke it fluently. The daughter admitted that she purposely spoke English when her father upset her because she knew it would frustrate and upset him.

Although what the daughter did was not nice, it illustrates that the language barrier is real.

In addition to the diversity of spoken languages, there are more than 310 religions and denominations in the United States. The odds of everyone in your classroom having the same religious beliefs or church affiliations are low. You must respect students' learned beliefs and not discriminate against them or force your beliefs on them.

The Myth of Color Blindness

Some educators believe that they are color blind and therefore don't need to increase their cultural awareness. Color blindness is the racial ideology that posits the best way to end discrimination is by treating individuals as equally as possible, without regard to race, culture, or ethnicity, notes Monica T. Williams (2011). Most Black and Latino males, who regularly encounter difficulties due to race, experience color blind ideologies quite differently. Colorblindness creates a society that denies their negative racial experiences, rejects their cultural heritage, and invalidates their unique perspectives (Williams, 2011).

It is generally white educators accustomed to a life of privilege who claim color blindness and do not realize the disservice they do to students of color who likely don't enjoy a life of privilege. By refusing to expand their understanding of the students who most need their support, they are missing the opportunity to inspire those students and possibly change the course of their lives.

Conclusion

Understanding culture is something that must take place at every K–12 school in the United States and abroad. I urge administrators to organize activities designed to help staff open up about their culture and beliefs—and have teachers engage in the same activities with students—to dispel the myth of color blindness and break down cultural barriers.

CHAPTER 2

Culturally Aware Teaching Practices

Imagine . . .

- Being frightened for your life instead of reassured when you see police officers.
- Coming home to a small, cramped apartment and being yelled at by your mother and her boyfriend and told there is no dinner for you.
- Going for an after-school snack only to find that the cabinets and refrigerator are completely bare.
- Getting harassed for being a good student and labeled as "acting white" by your friends with poor grades who pressure you to do things you don't want to do.
- Getting off your school bus after school and being robbed or assaulted on your way home or to play sports.
- Sitting in the classroom every day feeling helpless, confused, discriminated against, frustrated, alone, and hungry.
- Being in a class taught by a well-dressed, well-groomed, well-spoken white teacher who can't even begin to imagine what life is like for you.
- Daily living in fear because you don't know if your wallet will be mistaken for a gun.
- Giving 100 percent effort every day in class and, knowing that your teacher doesn't believe that you have the ability to learn, being confused and wondering whether you should keep trying.

- Coming into a school building every day knowing the leader of that building is not supporting you or your classmates who look like you.
- Being socially and economically disadvantaged and daily dealing with the stress that comes along with those realities.

Now imagine that a student dealing with all these issues is sitting in your classroom, walking through the hallways of your building, waiting to be inspired by a loving, caring, and trustworthy teacher or administrator. When that student leaves your classroom (or building) for the last time and moves on to the next grade (or school), will they remember you as the one who inspired them or will they remember you as the one who hindered them? Students always remember how you made them feel—whether it happened last week or 15 years ago.

Far too many educators haven't bridged the gap between themselves and their Black and Latino male students. They can't run down a list of these students' successes because they haven't been able to connect with them, despite being in the perfect position to serve as leaders and change agents in their lives. The disconnect, detrimental to students, is detrimental to teachers as well, leaving many feeling unfulfilled, burned out, and even resentful of the students who need them most.

In this chapter, I offer guidelines based on my years of experience as an inspirational teacher and administrator of young men of color. If you are having difficulty connecting with your Black or Latino male students, consciously incorporate these strategies into your practice and align your classroom and building procedures with them. These guidelines have served to greatly improve my teaching and school leadership and have enabled me to become "that" inspirational educator to my students. My hope is that they will do the same for you.

The Six Core Values for Teaching Black and Latino Males

If you keep the six core values for teaching Black and Latino males—love, trust, fairness, support, accountability, safety—foremost in mind as you implement the guidelines that follow, you'll be well on your way to becoming that "one caring teacher" to your students.

Love

Show your students that you love them:

- Love yourself enough to know that it is OK to care about your students' well-being.
- Love your students enough to make every effort to provide them with the best education possible.
- Love is a choice, not a feeling. Choose to love your students daily.
- Love always seeks the welfare of the other person; it does not seek to hurt people.
- Love sets aside beliefs, desires, and preferences and puts those of your students first.

Trust

Trust is

- Taking your student's word as truth.
- Acting in ways that make students feel they can place their trust in you.
- Giving a student a chance to get it right and believing he can do it.

- Leading by example by keeping your word and following through.
- Making recommendations with a student's input instead of issuing demands.

Fairness

Fairness is

- Treating all students in the same manner, regardless of race, socioeconomic status, or behavior issues.
- Not showing favoritism.
- Viewing all students as having the potential to do well.
- Giving all students the opportunity to be their best.
- Playing by the rules and not changing them to make it convenient for someone else.
- Listening with an open mind.

Support

Support your students by

- Honoring their choices and voices.
- Gaining an understanding of their truths.
- Offering encouragement.
- Listening without judging.
- Valuing their opinions.
- Having a short memory when they make mistakes.

Accountability

Accountability is

- Accepting responsibility for your behaviors and attitudes toward your Black and Latino male students and expecting your students to do the same.

- Admitting when you have made a mistake or have wrongfully accused or judged someone and expecting your students to do the same.
- Creating a mission statement for your building or classroom that is inclusive of all your students.
- Giving a concise explanation for your actions that helps everyone involved reach a resolution.
- For administrators, being responsible for the actions of the staff you hired.

Safety

Safety is

- Refraining from intimidating and manipulating your students.
- Being aware of and respecting the physical space of your students.
- Providing interventions for bullies and the students affected by their behavior.
- Recognizing students affected by trauma.
- Protecting and helping emotional students learn to control their emotions and giving them steps to deal with their temperamental issues.

Becoming Aware of Our Own Biases

In addition to the news media controlling some of our thought processes, many of us have learned bad habits through the years from relatives, friends, and others. No one is born a racist. No one is born hating themselves or others. No one is born with division in their heart. No one is born saying, "I don't want to be around certain people." All these behaviors are learned over time from the people we are surrounded by and from our experiences. Patterns of negative behavior are sometimes passed down from generation to generation—and passed along from colleagues and co-workers.

Making judgments about Black and Latino males is unfair to them. Be careful with your assumptions. They can slip into your decision making in the classroom with your students. They can slip into the culture of your building (if you are an administrator). Everyone has biases. Some more than others. Anytime I'm speaking to a group of educators at a professional development forum or at an education conference, I ask those in attendance to raise their hands if they have biases, and most everyone raises their hands. Then when I ask the same individuals to voluntarily state their biases, no hands are raised and everyone remains quiet. No one wants to share their biases (because most people don't want others to know their real biases), but students are unfairly exposed to and judged by them every day. When educators are not aware of the repercussions of their biases, they have the potential to be unfair and judgmental of students who do not fit into their definition of a "typical Black or Latino male student."

All educators have an idea of what their ideal student is like. Maybe he comes to class early, is well-prepared, raises his hand (even to respond to the toughest questions), studies for tests, makes good grades, participates in class, and doesn't talk or pass notes during class. Maybe an image comes to mind of what this student looks like based on past interactions with great students.

Then there are the typical students who come to class dealing with peer-pressure and home-life issues and social stresses. They exemplify characteristics of students deemed to be good. Educators are generally willing to work with them because they can easily see the possibility of the students succeeding in their classrooms. But what happens when a Black or Latino male student doesn't exemplify what you deem a good student to be? How is he being treated by you and your colleagues? Where do you see him going in the future? How empathetic are you to his needs? How much confidence do you have that he can be a great student?

I recently saw a cooking show featuring Martha Stewart and rapper and actor Snoop Dogg. If I asked someone who didn't know either of their backgrounds which one of them was a felon, most would likely say that it was Snoop—although Martha Stewart, not Snoop, is a felon. (I have seen Snoop Dogg on a few occasions, and each time he had marijuana smoke coming from some part of his body, but he is not a felon.) Looks can be very deceiving. What does a felon look like? Anyone from any walk of life can be a felon. Color doesn't matter. Felons come in all colors and genders. The media leads everyone to believe that felons are mostly men of color, but that is not necessarily true.

What Do You Think Based on What You See?

What are your thoughts when you see young men wearing sagging pants? Do you label them as thugs? Do you label them as uneducated? Do you group them with those who are violent and out of control? Most adults can remember following fads when they were young. There have been many of them through the years—parachute pants, Jordache jeans, greasy curls, curly perms, shags, Cross Colours, neon, big hair, mohawks, and so on. Whatever it was, we all went through phases and fads as students. Today, although some Black and Latino male students are inclined to sag their pants or wear dreadlocks or braids, it doesn't mean they are thugs, unintelligent, or bad students. Appearance alone should not result in a young man being labeled "not teachable."

Fresh off the football field after being cut by the NFL, when I began my teaching career in the mid-1990s, I wore my hair in braids.

In the same way that not everyone who wears a suit and has a business card is a businessman, not everyone who wears braids is a thug, unintelligent, or a bad student.

I teach young men to dress the way they would like to be addressed; please do the same. Be careful about telling a young man to "pull himself up by the bootstraps" (as many may find that difficult to do if they don't have bootstraps to pull up).

Change, But Only So Much

These young men can be chameleons. Although they adjust to their surroundings, it's tough for kids who come from an impoverished environment, who have learned the ways of their neighborhood, to conduct themselves in a completely different manner when they are in the school environment (which, in most cases, necessitates that their behavior be the polar opposite of how they are accustomed to behaving). Though some learn to adapt, others have a tough time turning it "on" and "off." When given the option, some kids choose to do whatever it takes to "fit in" in their neighborhoods because to them, the threat in the streets seems more severe than the repercussion of being disciplined in school. Keep in mind when assessing a student based on appearance, slang, or demeanor that intelligent students may pretend to know less than they do, which may result in them not meeting the visual expectations of the school and its administrators—or society as a whole.

Their Home Lives Travel with Them

A teacher once accused me of smoking marijuana because my clothes smelled like it when I came to school. My stepfather smoked marijuana, but I had never smoked it. Although the teacher who accused me never saw me smoke it, and I told her and the administrator that I'd never smoked it a day in my life, I was suspended from school for three days. It affected me in the worst way. I never forgot how I was treated.

Don't assume because a young man smells like marijuana or cigarettes that the student smokes. What if that student lives in a household where marijuana and cigarettes are smoked regularly by everyone else in the house except him? I didn't have a separate room to escape to, so the smell was in my clothes. I lost three days of learning because of someone else's bias.

Functioning While Surrounded by Dysfunction

If you have Black and Latino males who hang with other young men from their neighborhood who may get into trouble, it doesn't mean they want to get into trouble.

No teachers, pharmaceutical representatives, doctors, or lawyers lived in the neighborhood where I grew up. There were mostly blue-collar workers and "street pharmacists" (drug dealers, that is). I had friends who sold drugs. We all grew up playing together and having fun together.

We all hung out together, but I had my own goals and aspirations—running track and playing college football, getting a college degree, playing in the NFL, and starting my own business. Yet some educators stereotyped me because of the people I hung around.

Telling a young man with good grades whose family members drink, smoke, and do drugs not to go home or hang around with kids in his neighborhood who participate in "sketchy" activities is not productive. Where's he going to go? His home, regardless of the activities that may take place there, is still home to him, and you can't assume that he is participating in any illicit activities that may take place there. The people in his home are still family. They are the people he lives with. He may have an abusive stepfather or an uncle who drinks excessively, but he still wants to do well in school. His family dysfunction exists, but it doesn't change the fact that he is smart and intelligent. Once he is able to live on his own, he can then change the narrative of his life.

There is dysfunction of some sort in all families. Administrators, counselors, board members, and teachers all have dysfunction in their immediate or extended families. Although some dysfunction is more socially acceptable than others, it's still dysfunction. Some dysfunction is visible and some is hidden, but it's still dysfunction. When you become an educator who aspires to help students become great, your stereotypes and biases have to change even as you are coping with your own family's dysfunction. You may not always understand the dysfunction linked to a student's family. However, the teachers and administrators who reach students understand that beneath the layers is a child with the potential to do well and a child who wants to do well. A young man full of hope who is ready to change the narrative of his life.

You May Be Pleasantly Surprised

Kids will surprise you. They really want to succeed, no matter how they act in school. Some are just putting on a front to be tough in front of their friends, acting out to get attention. They're just trying to fit in. If you take the time to talk to your students, you will find out more about them than you might think.

Have one-on-one conversations. Once a relationship is built, one-on-one conversations are one of the best ways to get to know these young men. Their peers are not around to influence them and you will meet their authentic selves. There are some kids who just don't know who they are and need a boost of confidence. We can help in that area by speaking encouraging words to them.

Resist the urge to stereotype. I know a lot of educators who have eaten their words after falsely stereotyping me. The negative stereotypes fueled me to prove them wrong. Some of our students may not respond as I did. Your stereotypes and biases can be dream killers. If you choose to be open and accepting, you can become a dream restorer.

Listen. If a kid comes to school already on fire, you can either pour gasoline on him (escalating the situation) or pour water on him (diffusing the situation). When you pour gasoline on a student, he becomes more upset than he was already. (Sadly, I have witnessed educators pour gasoline on children already on fire and then write them up or kick them out of class and school.) However, when you pour water on a student—by listening, allowing him to vent, telling him that everything will be OK, and allowing him to work through his emotions—you and the student can work together to resolve the situation. Remember, you can't put out fire with fire.

Your Character and Daily Habits

Your character and daily habits shape you as a person. Your character is who you are when no one is watching. It's the kinds of conversations you have behind closed doors. It's the real, authentic you. What kind of jokes do you tell and listen to? Your daily habits are based on what you think on a daily basis. If you think Black and Latino students are criminals, that's how you will treat those students every day—whether consciously or unconsciously.

Peel Back the Onion

Black and Latino male students are just like other students you teach. They have problems. They have relationship issues with their parents and their significant others. Some come from tough circumstances and have trust issues. Some come from middle- or upper-class families yet have their share of issues and shortcomings. Once you peel back the onion, you will discover that all your students are good kids just trying to figure things out while dealing with the pressures of growing up in the world we live in today. They are no different than your own children. The things that they do wrong may not be as bad as we make them out to be.

Cultural Awareness and the Physical Environment

Classroom Routines and Setup

Classrooms with routines will be the most successful classrooms —and will best serve students who have experienced trauma. Have a daily routine that rarely changes and you will have a successful classroom. The atmosphere you create in your classroom will set the tone for the entire school year. Also, where you stand on the first day is extremely important. Consider the following:

- When do you take attendance?
- What words do you share at the beginning of class?
- Is homework due right away?
- Do you give a quiz at the beginning of class?

Consistency is important. When students know their routines and know what to expect every day, they tend to be more comfortable in that environment, and behavioral issues are minimized.

Having a seating chart cuts down on confusion or friends sitting with friends. It also forces students to get to know their classmates. Start off your class by allowing different students to take on leadership roles (e.g., passing out papers, taking attendance, collecting assignments). The exit strategy for the day should be taken seriously and should be the same every day. Consider the following:

- Do you allow the last five minutes of class for questions or concerns? or
- When the bell rings, does everyone scatter?

The way you set up the chairs is extremely important. While a consistent classroom style has proven to be beneficial in most settings, depending on the personalities of your students, sometimes change is good. Whatever you determine is your routine, try to stick to it every day.

Also, be consistent in the words you speak as these young men enter your classroom. Because these students bring with them stresses from home, baggage, peer pressure, and hopes for the future and have little direction, their first exchange with their leader is important.

Routines That Help Students Feel Safe

It is paramount that you create an orderly, routine environment. Many Black and Latino males living in difficult circumstances crave routine because it helps them to feel safe. Knowing exactly what to expect day in and day out reduces their anxiety. Every educator should have a routine that makes their students feel comfortable and safe.

Some classroom routines that help students feel comfortable and safe are as follows:

- Involving students in developing classroom rules.
- Posting your daily schedule so students know what to expect.
- Letting students know when class will be taught by a substitute teacher.
- Giving students specific jobs and assignments (post and rotate names).

- Establishing routines for entering and exiting the classroom.
- Having a routine in place for restroom breaks.
- Having a routine to follow when school work is finished early.
- Establishing a routine for classroom cleanup.
- Having a routine for free time, talk time, and so on.

Setting the Tone

Tone should be established on day one.

You will always set the tone for your classroom and building. Make students feel comfortable. Start your day with a smile and saying things like, "It's going to be a great year." School will be these students' home for the next several months. Many may spend more time at school than at home.

Wall colors. What you put on your walls is extremely import-ant. Colors schemes are significant. Colorful schemes tend to keep the attention of students. Colors can make a room feel warm and inviting. According to the article "Colors in the Classroom Learning Environment—Color Your World" (https://smithsystem.com/resource-library/article-library /color-world/), color plays an important role in emotion, productivity, communication, and learning. Color has a direct link to positive and negative learning. Carefully consider the colors of the walls, desks, tables, and chairs. Also, ensure that classroom photos reflect the various cultures and ethnicities of your students.

Messages. Your messages should be positive and affirming.

I once walked into a classroom and saw posted on a wall, "IT'S YOUR TEMPER, PLEASE KEEP IT." I couldn't believe that someone would actually post such a message in a school environment. How would you feel if you walked in and saw this on the wall of a classroom you were supposed to learn in? When a student is already coming in with his own insecurities and issues at home, that is the last thing he needs to see to make him feel safe. This message basically says, "We don't care about your state of mind. In fact, just keep it to yourself." I would feel disturbed in this classroom. I would also feel unwelcomed, unsafe, and unable to share with my teacher if I'm upset or unhappy about anything. It sends a strong, wrong message to students. It should never become the norm.

Another post in this same classroom read, "THINGS HAPPEN FOR A REASON, SO WHEN I REACH OVER AND SMACK YOU UPSIDE THE HEAD, JUST REMEMBER . . . YOU GAVE ME A REASON!" Though some people may find humor in such a sign, others may find it painful. Young men of color are, unfortunately, used to being mistreated and many come in with chips on their shoulders. This post could be the very thing that sets a student off. Such misguided use of words pours gasoline on students who are already on fire.

As the messages on the wall of a classroom or school building are being absorbed daily by developing minds, be sure to make them positive and uplifting.

Debunking Sensationalism and Misinformation

A great majority of all the stories in the news about our Black and Latino males are negative. I asked a friend who is a news anchor why so many stories in the news are negative, especially those pertaining to Black and Latino males. She responded by saying that when the stories are about violence and negativity, the ratings go up and that when positive stories are reported, the ratings go down. This is very sad, but true. She also said it was sad that when negative stories led the news, the producers most always led with the faces of Black and Latino males.

Is there any positive news about our young men of color out there? Of course there is. However, stories about Black and Latino males are only considered newsworthy if someone is shot, stabbed, or killed. With such a consistent influx of negative reports, some educators have developed a fear of these young men. Their perception has become their reality. Some are just scared to admit that they react to these young men based on fear and frustration stemming from what they hear. The news will cause you to be scared. Sound and images are extremely powerful. People are conditioned to believe what they see and hear. If I keep watching the news, I'm going to be scared of myself when I look in the mirror.

Some educators take this misleading information and presume the worst about innocent students and don't even give them a chance to show who they are as individuals. When educators bring learned biases into the classroom, it dilutes the learning environment. Sadly, students continue to fail because they are subject to educators' biases.

The sensationalism of the latest news stories involving criminal activity can be frightening and is one of the main reasons many educators are biased toward Black and Latino male students. If you watch the news every day, try skipping a day or two—you won't miss much. The stories are the same. The news highlights a few bad apples as though they represent an entire race. Though in reality only 2 percent of Black and Latino males commit violent crimes, the media would have you believe that the 98 percent who are working and trying to get home to their families are committing violent crimes. As Black-on-Black crime is real—90.1 percent of crimes against Black men are committed by Black men—so too is white-on-white crime—83.5 percent of crimes against white people are committed by white people. The same is true of Hispanics and Latinos. Most of the violent crimes committed by any race are committed by someone of that same race (Harriot, 2017).

Statistics show that there are more Black and Latino males in college than in prison; do your best as an educator to ensure that this remains the case. Set high expectations for these students and expect them to do well.

Avoid Microaggressions

Racial microaggressions are daily indirect, subtle, or unintentional messages that communicate hostile, derogatory, negative slights and insults against racial or ethnic minorities. Some messages, though intended as compliments, are actually insults. For example:

- **"You are a credit to your race."** This statement is tactless, demeaning, and anything but a compliment. There are good and bad people of *every* race. How does someone become a credit to their race by just doing the right thing? Why can't he be a credit to society and the world instead of his race? Compliment people as you would want to be complimented. Say, "Good job," "Excellent work," or "I'm proud of you."

- **"Wow, you speak good English!"** Don't assume that Black students who speak colloquially among themselves don't know how to speak more formally, or that students of Latin-American descent aren't native English speakers. Such assumptions reflect a bias based purely on stereotypes and not on the individual being addressed.

- **"When I see you, I don't see color."** People come in a wide range of hues. If you are in any diverse setting, there will be color. I don't know anyone who doesn't see color every day. People from different races don't want their color ignored, they just want it to be respected. It's OK for you to see color. It's OK to acknowledge color. Although it's not a crime or an insult to see color, it's an insult to say you don't see it when in fact you do. I see color every day and it's OK that you do, too. (See "The Myth of Color blindness" in Chapter 1.)

- **"You're different from them. I know you."** When someone befriends a person of a different race, they get to know them as an individual. They may even begin to feel comfortable in their presence. However, that same person undermines the friendship when they discuss the actions of individuals who are of their friend's race who have committed a crime or done something despicable or demeaning and end by telling the friend, "But you're different from them. I know you." Such a comment, though probably meant to be a compliment, is really an insult. Putting down an entire race but singling out the person who you know as the one decent person in the race is deplorable and narrow-minded.

Lead by Example

Help to educate colleagues who view cultural awareness negatively. Don't participate in the negative conversations about young men of color. Speak out if you hear racist comments. Share tools you've learned. Understand how negative stereotypes have shaped others' thinking.

Lead by example. Talk to your colleague about a time when you felt discriminated against. Then talk to that same colleague about a time when you made an inappropriate remark about someone of another race or culture. Encourage staff to participate in cultural awareness workshops or share information about their cultures with students and each other.

Helpful Resources

Following are suggested texts on diversity and culturally responsive teaching:

- *50 Literacy Strategies for Culturally Responsive Teaching, K–8* by Patricia Ruggiano Schmidt and Wen Ma
- *Culturally Responsive Standards-Based Teaching: Classroom to Community and Back* (2nd edition) by Steffen Saifer, Keisha Edwards, Debbie Ellis, Lena Ko, and Amy Stuczynski
- *Responsive Teaching: Cognitive Science and Formative Assessment in Practice* by Harry Fletcher-Wood
- *Culturally Responsive Teaching: Theory, Research, and Practice* by Geneva Gay
- *Addressing Diversity in Schools: Culturally Responsive Pedagogy* by Heraldo V. Richards, Ayanna F. Brown,

and Timothy B. Forde (http://www.niusileadscape.org/
docs/FINAL_PRODUCTS/NCCRESt/practitioner_
briefs/%95%20TEMPLATE/DRAFTS/AUTHOR%20
revisions/annablis%20pracbrief%20templates/Diversity_
Brief_highres.pdf)

Experiencing Bias

When I first started teaching high school in the mid-1990s, I wasn't fully ready for what I would face. Having been recently cut from the NFL (Minnesota Vikings) during training camp, I came off the football field and walked into a classroom with my own anxieties, regret, anger, disappointments, and shortcomings. I wore my hair in cornrows, braids, or an afro when I taught. Some days, especially in the beginning of my career, I didn't want to be there.

I dressed and wore my hair then based on how I felt at the time. Once I realized that most kids today dress and wear their hair based on how they feel, I realized that in dealing with my students, I was dealing with myself.

When I went to my job interview to get the teaching job, the panel stared at me for several minutes before saying a word. Their perception of me had become their reality until they started examining my credentials (a graduate of Western Kentucky University, I was enrolled in graduate school at the time and had a 3.5 GPA). One of the panelists repeatedly looked down at my résumé and back up at me. His implicit biases were very apparent.

When I saw the panelist blatantly processing who I was, I couldn't help but think, "Just because someone wears their hair in braids or in an afro doesn't mean that they are thugs or criminals." It didn't mean I didn't have the credentials to do the job effectively. Young men are rebellious. My hairstyle was "in" back then. I wondered if I would be denied an opportunity because of my outward appearance. I could tell that the panelist was wrestling with the fact that I had the credentials but there was no way I could be the person on the paper in front of him based on what I looked like in his eyes. He couldn't hide his feelings and thoughts.

After a stellar interview, I got the job. However, once on the job, I was subject to a colleague's perceptions.

On my first day, I was taken to the office by another teacher who thought I was one of the students who was late to class. She told me to go get a late pass. Although I explained to her that I was a new teacher and was on my prep period, she insisted on taking me to the office anyway. Nothing I said to her convinced her that I was a teacher. I eventually gave in so she would stop making a scene in front of the students and staff. When we got to the office, the principal said to her, "Let go of Mr. Jackson's arm."

The teacher's perception convinced her that I was a student. Maybe your perception of a student based on his appearance leads you to assume that a student is a nuisance, a trouble-maker, nonchalant, mean, or will be a problem in your class before you have even given him a chance.

Be mindful of your assumptions because if you don't allow yourself to see who that student really is, you will only see what you expect to see or what you see on television or on social media or hear during inappropriate conversations with family members, friends, or colleagues.

Fighting Biases as a Teacher

I didn't understand my position and who I was as an educator when I first started teaching, but I'm reminded daily when I see my former students that I matter and that my work impacted their lives in a positive way.

I hadn't planned on teaching. I planned on playing in the NFL for 10 years, but 10 years turned into more like 10 days. I was cut, and my NFL dreams were crushed. After a short depression, I found myself looking for a job and ran into the superintendent of the school district I had worked in who told me they were looking for an industrial technology teacher. Although industrial technology was my major, I wasn't ready to teach it—especially in a classroom. Teaching wasn't on my list of goals and objectives.

During my first three months of teaching, I almost quit. I didn't think I could take it. Students were so disrespectful, and I didn't handle disrespect well. My mom raised me to respect adults, but some of the Black and Latino male students I worked with daily weren't raised the same way. They talked back and were defiant and very angry. They would curse me out, show up late for class, half do their work, make scenes, and so on. I wanted to retaliate but knew those young men were dealing with issues that had nothing to do with me. In fact, I took myself back to my teenage years and thought about how hurt I was at that age and how I was quick to anger. I passed on to the young men I worked with what I had learned over the years—a man slow to anger is a wise man.

I had to learn how to control my emotions. As an adult, I used to let student's behavior get to me, forgetting that I had control of my own emotions and responses. I had to better understand that outside of securing a student's attention, teaching and guiding our students into a brighter and more hopeful future was one of our most important tasks. Relationships needed to be built. Healing needed to take place in their lives and mine. You can't put out fire with fire.

My colleagues thought because my kids looked like me that I had it easy, but I didn't. (Just as one white person doesn't speak for all white people and one Hispanic person doesn't speak for all Hispanic people, one Black person doesn't speak for all Black people.) I had my own struggles. But I eventually turned my selfish thoughts filled with self-pity into a competitive drive to change the mindsets of all my students. The Latino population was growing rapidly, and I wanted to make sure I was an example and leader to all my Black and Latino male students (the vast majority of my students).

I educated myself on Latino culture. I found that those Latino young men were dealing with their own issues (the threat of deportation, families being separated, English as a second language, etc.), and I understood that "in order to educate the mind, you must capture the heart." I also had to deal with my own issues, insecurities, and shortcomings, including the stereotypes that I associated with the young men I worked with.

Conclusion

You have to be mentally tough to be a teacher. You have to exercise resolve, patience, and restraint. Some educators interact with 40 to 150 different personalities daily, which is tough and challenging within itself. Once you add all the paperwork, politics, job cuts, low salaries, and lack of camaraderie, teaching becomes unattractive to those who lose sight of their mission.

My former students are still in contact with me today because I showed them a different way that helped them in school and in life outside the school. When I run into students now, I feel the same fulfillment that I felt when I taught them.

CHAPTER 3

Core Beliefs and Mindsets of a
Culturally Responsive Educator

If your students described you in one word, what would that one word be? Loving? Strict? Passive? Stubborn? Helpful? Angry? Abrasive? Nice? Sweet? Mean? Nonchalant?

Ask yourself, "How do my students view me?" If your students view you as mean and abrasive, they will more than likely shut down and not want to learn from you. Maybe you know that your students see you as strict, abrasive, or boring, but you think students need strong discipline and boundaries to ensure learning (which is not always the case). As an educator, I felt that I was too strict at times because I judged everyone by the acts of a few. Maybe because there is so much stress in education and so much content to cover, you feel it's OK to be strict, abrasive, or boring. Maybe you've heard other educators say it's OK because "those kids" have trouble learning anyway. It is imperative to turn your gaze inward and question what limiting and biased beliefs you have about students and teaching that are disadvantaging kids. It's not always the students. Sometimes it's the teachers.

Who Are You?

I was speaking at a school assembly once when a student shouted out, "Who are you, Mr. Jackson?" I immediately replied, "I am, first and foremost, a man of God. I am a husband, a father, a son, a brother, an educator, a coach, a mentor, a national speaker, a consultant, an author, a game-changer,

a community leader, a hard worker, a servant, and a hustler."
(Note: By *hustler* I mean *go-getter*. There is nothing wrong
with being a hustler as long as you hustle honestly and with
good intent.) When someone ask you who you are, you should
be able to answer immediately. Take a moment and write
down eight to 10 words that describe you.

Know Your "Why"

You must know your "why." Your reasons for teaching will help
you get through the tough days. When you understand who
you are and why you teach, you become more patient, you're
able to show more constraint, and you're more effective and
happy as a teacher.

Ask yourself the following questions:

- Why am I a teacher?
- Why am I an administrator?
- What is my "why"?
- Why do I do what I do?
- What is the one area of my life that I need to improve
  upon to help me better understand and work more
  effectively with Black and Latino males?
- What can I do to build stronger relationships with my
  Black and Latino male students?
- What three words would my students use to
  describe me?
- How do I want my students to remember me?

In this chapter, I'm going to ask you to really get to know
yourself as an education professional. This chapter outlines the
core beliefs and mindsets necessary to best serve all students

and support your Black and Latino male students. It will challenge you to reflect on how you've developed certain beliefs and mindsets. As you read this chapter, reaffirm your commitment to these values—and to your students.

Be Caring

If you don't feel like your students are going to be great students simply because you're their teacher, show your students that you care—that's half the battle. There is no perfect educator out there. Everyone has flaws. Having empathy will give you what it takes to turn any student around. Are you that one caring adult whom your students need to hear from daily? Are you speaking success into your Black and Latino male students? Claim your students as your success stories, and they will never forget it or you. Treat them like they are yours, and they will follow you and believe in you.

Commit fully. Becoming "that" caring adult comes with a responsibility. You must be fully committed, even on your bad days. Some days you won't feel like coming to work, but you have to do it anyway. Many of us have our own kids and our own issues, but our students still deserve the best we can give them. Even when Black and Latino male students get on your last nerve, you must speak positive words into their spirits and teach them with care.

Don't feel sorry for them. Caring means having empathy for your students without feeling sorry for them. When you feel sorry for students, your expectations of them are lowered. Students need your expectations to remain high. Don't show favoritism. All students deserve to have you believe in them.

When they go out into the real world, they will be competing with the rest of the world, despite their circumstances. It is your job to care enough to teach these young men how to handle adversity as well as success and how to be respectful, disciplined, accountable, and confident in who they are.

Be Open

At a recent presentation to more than 600 New Jersey 5th and 6th graders, I asked any students who were in pain to stand up, and almost every student stood up. I then asked students who were angry to stand, and more than half of the students stood up. These were 11- and 12-year-olds. I asked how many of them felt misunderstood by their teachers and administrators and, again, almost every student stood up. And when I asked how many of them had contemplated suicide, well over half of them stood up.

These students were open with me because I shared some of my deepest hurts with them and let them know that I'm not perfect and have made many mistakes along the way. Those mistakes have made me who I am today. I was kicked out of school on more than one occasion. I got into fights growing up. I hung with the wrong crowd at times in my life. I lost some so-called friends who turned out to be haters. As a teenager, after my friend Tony was murdered, I feared the same fate and carried a loaded weapon for protection. Being open about my life helped me build a strong bond with my students. They needed to see my human side.

I still use my stories to teach students and educators the importance of not allowing trauma or mistakes to define them. I am a survivor of sexual and physical abuse, and discussing this trauma with my students was an empowering moment of owning my past hurts to move forward in life. By being open in that way, I was able to help a 16-year-old young lady who had been molested by her stepfather since she was nine years old (resulting in her stepfather being arrested and later sentenced to 15 years in prison). If I had not shared my story, she may not have been able to find the strength to come forward or to find closure. Students will open up to you when you share who you really are. Although males can sometimes be stubborn and may not trust people enough to share their most inner thoughts and hurts, if you are open with them as you work to build relationships and rapport with them, they will open up—eventually.

Do you have personal stories you'd be willing to share with students if you knew they could make a difference in their lives? It takes bravery to open up, but it can make all the difference.

Be Humble

You can't live in your humility and your pride at the same time. The two can't coexist. You must make a choice. No one can make you be humble. You must choose to be humble. Many educators live in their pride. You are living in your pride if you are

- Self-centered
- Arrogant
- Easily offended
- Always upset

- Bitter
- Hurt
- Timid

> When you are hurt and timid, you are focusing on yourself and not others. (When I was hurt, all I discussed was my hurt, and I couldn't get past it to help others in pain.) It's a problem when your inability to get past your hurt is an obstacle for students who may need to share their hurts with you. Being timid is living in your pride because you must at times be assertive with your students, which will require you to step out of your comfort zone and look from the outside in.

Remove yourself from the center. No one can make you be humble. You must make that choice yourself. Becoming aware requires you to remove yourself from the center. When a young man offends you, remove yourself from the center and don't play the victim. You will no longer be offended or hurt because you understand that kids are coming in with baggage and trust issues and that it takes time to build bonds with them. You understand that it's not about you. Kids can say what they want, but you know they are lashing out in fear and not at you.

Teaching is for the humble, not the prideful. Tell yourself that you will live in your humility and not in your pride so you can be a better role model for your students. Teaching alone will humble you: it's very rewarding, but it's also very tough. In addition to understanding students who deal with trauma, we have to attend meetings we don't always want to attend, keep our lesson plans on task whether everyone understands or not, prepare students for ongoing standardized tests, and deal with parents who don't always come in peace.

One day I was teaching a class and one of my students kept talking to another student while I was teaching a lesson. I let it slide for a little while, but the talking continued and got intense. Finally, I yelled out to the student, "Cut it out." He yelled back at me, and I asked him to step out in the hallway. He stormed out, slamming the door, and kept walking when I called him.

My first mistake was when I lost my cool and took it personally when this student was talking in my class. I was in my pride and not in my humility. I never asked him what he was talking about. (When I later found out from another student that his brother had been murdered over the weekend, I felt horrible.) I felt bad about raising my voice when I'd told my students that raising your voice doesn't solve anything or make a situation better.

When I ran into the young man as I was leaving school that day, I apologized to him for the way I responded to him talking in my class and told him that I was sorry to hear about his brother. He looked as though he wasn't used to being either talked to in a caring manner or apologized to. I saw a glimpse of light in his face. He wasn't expecting an apology, which made him feel better and that someone cared. I was thankful that I was able repair the situation while it was still fresh. Our relationship remained strong long after that incident.

Returning to my humility allowed me to apologize to him. I had to take a step back and look at myself, which most of us don't like to do, especially when kids are involved.

Who do *you* need to apologize to for losing your cool? How many times have you yelled at students after encouraging them to handle conflict differently? Although we can't go back in time, we can humbly move forward with a renewed spirit and mindset.

Know and Work on Your Shortcomings

The first step to personal growth is honesty. We must be honest with ourselves about what we need to improve upon. Throughout my teaching career, I had many things to work on and improve. Whether it's lack of patience, lack of understanding of race and culture, dealing with your own biases, being quick-tempered, or yelling a lot, make a concerted effort to know and work on your shortcomings.

Take a moment and list areas in your teaching life where you think you can improve. (Take this exercise, which will require you to let your guard down and be completely honest with yourself, seriously because your shortcomings could be holding you back from doing your job more efficiently.) Then write down how you plan to address the most pressing of your weaknesses. If you don't know how to overcome one or more of your shortcomings, seek further assistance and advice from your supervisor or counseling services in your area.

Holding on to Things and Being Quick to Anger

One of my shortcomings was that I had a tough time letting things go—especially when a student was blatantly disrespectful.

One day, a young Hispanic student called me a bitch in front of the whole class (of 36 students, most of whom were Black and Latino males). He then moved toward me as though he was going to physically attack me. The next day, I gave him a chance to get it right: I acted as nicely and professionally toward him as I did to my other students.

I was deeply bothered that the student was bold enough to have called me a bitch. Although I had trained my brain to have a short memory, the word lingered, and it was tough for me to move on. I had to remember the words I used to describe myself, and that word was not one that I used. I had to remember that this young man was coming from a tough background, where that word was used on a daily basis.

When I asked him why he was so comfortable using that word, he replied that his father told him that all Black people are bad. (His cousin had been killed by a Black man.) I told him his father was wrong and that, just as not all Hispanic young men are the same, not all Black people commit violent crimes. I then asked him to give me a chance.

He learned from his father that it was all right to be disrespectful to Black people. I told him that the language was not going to be tolerated in my classroom and that relationships are built on trust and honesty. He eventually gave me a chance, and our relationship grew strong. (When he later joked about having call me "that" name, I chuckled as I asked him to leave the incident in the past.)

Remember that it's important to renew your mind daily. Everyone deserves a second chance. Raise your hand if you ever made a mistake as a teacher or administrator. Didn't someone give you a second chance? You are still hanging in there. These young men are going to make mistakes. They are kids. They deserve to be forgiven. It's up to us to work on controlling our emotions and not taking things personally. My response to someone else's emotional response is up to me.

Holding on to offenses, both minor and major, can affect your health. In my case, doing so affected my blood pressure. I was diagnosed with hypertension more than 18 years ago. Eighteen years later, my blood pressure is under control—without the help of medication. My stress level is not a factor because I don't get stressed out anymore. I learned how to let things go. I learned to leave work at work.

I also came to terms with the reality that life happens. People will come into your life for a season and leave after a time. Bad things, as well as good things, will happen from time to time, but *you* control how you will respond. I changed my thought process. I am still a work in progress. I work to remain in peace at all, which means I need to stay away from certain educators who like to keep things going. I work to not become consumed by the issues of life. I work to move past petty disagreements in order to stay focused on more important matters. With time, it has required less and less effort. I spend time on myself by working out, eating right, getting rest, and meditating daily. Self-help is a must.

Another shortcoming I possessed was being quick to anger. This stemmed from the trauma I experienced as a kid and young adult growing up. Not having a father, living in poverty, and being bullied a lot in my neighborhood resulted in me being frustrated and angry. As an adult, I didn't initially realize the effects that anger continued to have on me. People would mention it to me, but I still didn't get it. If someone mentions it to you, it's time for you to take a look in the mirror without being defensive. My frustration and anger affected me, my students, my family, my job, and my relationships.

Steps to Overcoming Shortcomings

I overcame my anger in four steps:

1. *I admitted that I was angry.* This step, though the hardest, was the most important step—because many of us walk around in denial. Own up to your shortcomings.
2. *I wrote down everything I was upset about.* This helped me release that anger from my spirit and my body. I wrote about the abuse, the bullying, the letdowns, the robberies, the hurts and disappointments, how racism affected me, and so on. When I wrote it down, I released that negative energy from my spirit. It's very important to rid yourself of negative energy.
3. *I spoke to someone I trusted.* I spoke to my mentor and a few trusted colleagues about this issue and received some sound advice. Ray Satterfield, one of my trusted mentors, told me that my story was still being written and that going through tough situations would only benefit me by making me a stronger person who was qualified to help others. He encouraged me to talk about my issues and to never hold on to them (which helped me tremendously in my walk of healing). Ray also encouraged me to choose to be happy and peaceful, despite what I was going through.
4. *I forgave myself.* After I forgave myself for getting so angry, I forgave those who I felt caused my anger—though,

in reality, I caused my own anger (because, no matter who made me angry, how I controlled my emotions and my response was up to me).

To overcome your shortcomings, you must first admit that you have them. Face them one at a time. Not only will you become a better educator, you will become a happier person. Whether your shortcomings are that you show anger, are too timid, or have implicit biases, write them down on a piece of paper or type them on your computer and face them one at a time. After you record them, have an honest conversation with yourself. You can lie to anyone, but only you know the truth. After you master this technique, teach it to your students and your children.

Believe in *Every* Student

I believe the same thing today that I did when I began in education as a classroom teacher almost 25 years ago: every student can be a success story. Whether male, female, Black, Latino, white, Mexican, Native American, Middle Eastern, Asian, Indian, or what have you, every student has the potential to be great, and every student deserves a champion.

I had to believe that all my students could be successes before they could believe it for themselves. Students don't always know their full potential. It's up to us as educators to convince them that they can change their narrative. Many students come to school broken and lacking direction. Some have no idea that all they have to do is focus—block out the noise and negativity in their lives and focus on what they can control—and they can succeed at anything. Controlling responses to others is part of that process. People can do or say whatever they want to a person, but how a person responds is up to them.

Coach and Encourage

Your students need the right coaching and encouragement from the right educator. I taught my students how to write their own life stories the way they wanted them to go and believe in their own abilities, despite their current home situations. I taught them that the only place success comes before work is in the dictionary. Putting in the work always pays off! I taught them that their choices, not the color of their skin, would define their future success. I taught them that their family dysfunction was not their dysfunction. I taught them that their words would dictate their futures—if you want to be great, speak greatness over your life. The words that you speak should reflect the greatness over your life that you seek.

My words translated into results, and results translated into success stories that I used as reference points with incoming students who didn't believe in themselves. It's all a part of a positive cycle that I used repeatedly with my students, and the success stories continued: Kirk Hawkins, Jeremy Coleman, Tavares Harney, William Gooch (RIP), Ben Herman, Randy Cross, Brian Dinkins, and many others.

Educators, your words will dictate the future success or failure of every one of your students. You must believe that for yourself. Working in education isn't for everyone. You have to change your thought process. You can't believe what you see or hear on television. I didn't say there wouldn't be bumps in the road along the way. I didn't say that students won't come in acting out. I never said that every student will learn at the same speed or that every student will get it. I *did* say that despite their background and circumstances, every student has the potential to be a success story! Change your thought process and word choices to reflect this idea if that is what you truly believe.

Our job is to speak life into situations that seem to have no solutions. Speak hope into the hopeless. Believe in the unbelievable. Too many have given up on these Black and Latino males—including their own parents—but we should never give up on them. Where would we be if someone didn't believe in us or everyone gave up on us? Our words and leadership should be the example. Even if you feel like you've got it all together, temperature-check your students and staff from time to time to get their thoughts and opinions. Sometimes we must look in the mirror and ask ourselves, "Am I doing this effectively?"

Help Them Find Their Greatness

Again, *all* students have the ability to be great—and *you* have the ability to help them find their greatness. We often miss out on that opportunity when we don't dig deeper beyond the learned behaviors from home that might hide intellectual capabilities. What some students learn at home or in their community may at times hinder their ability to display their intelligence. Because in some homes children are told to shut up when they are inquisitive and simply want to know the answers, by the time they arrive in your classroom, they have been conditioned to not ask. They feel that they aren't worthy of knowing the answer or that their answer doesn't matter.

In some circles, being intelligent is looked down on and considered uncool. Some of your most intelligent students are hiding behind an exterior wall of fear that if they show what they really are capable of, they will lose their acceptance with friends. It's important to show them that it's OK to be smart by rewarding them for their intelligence (e.g., giving them prizes for correct answers or high scores on tests) and encouraging them to continue to be great. Let them know the benefits of intelligence (e.g., opportunities to excel academically and socially, earning the respect of other people, better quality of life) and the downside of associating with individuals who discourage them from showing their intelligence.

Knowing that regardless of circumstances they can graduate and even go to college is a real motivator, so make sure your students believe it. An ongoing conversation with students can help. Even extremely resistant students, when given the proper motivation, can learn to adjust to the academic environment in the same way that they adjust to their responsibilities at home.

Putting It into Practice

Here are some strategies to help you reflect, develop, and reinforce the beliefs and mindsets described in this chapter.

Focus on the Impact of Your Work

People who make a positive impact on others

- Commit to improving themselves.
- Are open and build relationships through connecting and sharing their knowledge.
- Uplift others as they rise.
- Understand that achieving their goal is not a single moment but the journey as a whole.
- Don't take it personally when a student has a bad day.
- Speak positive words to their students every day.

To make an impact, you must be willing to do more than is expected of you—including things that aren't in your job description. The recommendations in this book aren't in the teacher or administrator handbooks or in typical job descriptions. They reflect a holistic mindset of caring, focused on impact rather than a series of boxes to be checked. When you care, your heart will tell you what you need to do.

Here are a few tools to assist the students you work with when you care:

- Have an open-door policy whereby students can speak to you outside the classroom about problems they are dealing with.
- Have extra snacks on hand (e.g., apples, oranges, chips, etc.) and offer them to students daily. Some kids come to school hungry and will almost never let you know how hungry they really are.
- Provide ways students can communicate with you after school hours (e.g., e-mail, Twitter, Instagram) in case they need someone to lean on or for advice.
- Attend sporting events and other activities that students are involved in. Wave at them and make sure they see you in the stands. Doing this will help you build a stronger relationship with them.
- Have a time during class when students can discuss current events from their perspectives.
- Allow students to talk and vent, and be a good listener (that is, have an open dialogue without saying a lot).

I always look for e-mails after my presentations from participants because the impact left on them is important to the work that I do. It drives my work. Feedback is an indispensable component of any learning process. When I occasionally get an e-mail from someone who didn't particularly care for my presentation, I don't get offended. Rather, I take the time to explain what I meant so that the individual can come to some understanding. Sometimes people interpret things the wrong way and other times they just flat out don't agree with your thinking, and that's OK. No one knows it all, and no one is perfect. Not everyone will receive you the same way or agree with you—whether students, teachers, administrators, or parents—but the goal is to get the best out of students. Because our impact on them will affect what we get out of them, it must remain positive—no matter what.

Whether you chose the teaching profession or it chose you, what matters most is the impact you have on your students and staff. I didn't plan to be in this profession. I wanted to do something altogether different but ultimately found my way into teaching, coaching, and leading other people. Whatever the reason, we are here and our students and staff need us to be fully present without bias or malice. That means you must leave home at home and school at school. You must check your attitude at the door daily. A responsibility accompanied whatever motivated you to get into this profession.

Self-Evaluate

Self-evaluation, one of the hardest things to do, needs to take place every day. At the end of each day as an educator, I evaluated my teaching style and lesson plans. We should evaluate ourselves daily, because each day brings new challenges, new adventures, and new rewards. Each of us as educators needs to know how we did—good or bad—so that corrections and adjustments can be made. I get excited at the thought of improving and working on myself.

There will be some days that you feel like you did everything wrong. But once you evaluate what you did, you may realize that it wasn't as bad as you thought it was. Don't be so hard on yourself. Like many new educators, I was scared and nervous on my first day of teaching. I didn't know a lot of things, but I knew I cared about my students. I knew I had their best interests at heart.

Consider the following when evaluating yourself:

- What did I do today that positively impacted my students? Be specific.
- What did I do today that affirmed myself and my well-being? Be specific.
- What was the most challenging part of my day, and how do I fix it? Be specific.
- How was my communication style today, and what can I do to improve it?
- How would my students describe me in one word today? Why?
- How did I want to be perceived by my students today? Why?
- How was my rapport with my colleagues today, and what can I do to improve it?

Create a Mission Statement

A mission statement is a brief description of one's fundamental purpose. You should have a professional mission statement that you can always refer to. Your students should know your mission statement. It should be visible for everyone to see in your classroom or building. Administrators, those who enter your building should know what your mission statement is.

It should be prominently posted. It should be recited daily so everyone understands what your school or class stands for.

When creating your mission statement, you must keep in mind your values and beliefs. Following is the mission statement of Mountain Gap Middle School:

> The mission of Mountain Gap Middle School is to provide each student a diverse education in a safe, supportive environment that promotes self-discipline, motivation, and excellence in learning.

Your mission statement should inspire creativity, cultivate academic growth, and nurture diverse inclusion in your school or classroom. It should paint a picture that reminds you of your daily objectives and expresses who you are as a school district, school, classroom, and education professional. It is the voice representing you when you're not present. It shares with your students, their parents, and others what values you stand on and for. When you get frustrated, read your mission statements to remind you why you do the work that you do. (Trust me when I say that once you start dealing with the politics of the school system, you will need to recall your mission statement.)

What is your personal brand? How do you want to be represented? What kind of tone are you setting or not setting? Without a mission statement, your students will default to values and goals inconsistent with your own. Don't allow your students to walk the halls of your school and populate the classroom lost and without direction. If you have a solid mission statement, introduce it early and share it often—making it easier for colleagues and students to adapt to. Your mission statement sets the tone and guides your expectations. When you have a strong mission statement, no one will wonder who you are or what you stand for. No one will be confused about your values. No one will question the direction of your school, school district, or classroom.

Take a few moments and write a mission statement for your building or classroom; it should embody everything you stand for. Once you have written your mission statement, make sure everyone has a clear understanding of it, your vision, and what you want to accomplish. Afterward, have your students write mission statements that outline what they would like to accomplish in the school year. Administrators, have your staff—whether secretaries, custodians, teachers, or paraprofessionals—write mission statements as well and allow them to review and revise them in the middle of the school year and at the end of the year.

Speak Positivity into Your Spirit

Before you even step foot into the classroom or school building, speak positive words into your own spirit with self-affirmations such as

- I'm *that* one caring adult my students need for success.
- I will be the best educator I can be.
- I find fulfillment in being an educator.
- My work makes a difference.
- I love and appreciate my students and staff.
- My students succeed because of my guidance and leadership.
- I am a great educator who cares.
- I am smart.
- I can do all things.
- Every student can be a success story.

- I will block out negative advice and avoid negative people.
- My leadership makes a difference.
- I work hard on behalf of my students and staff.
- I believe in my ability to be a change agent.
- I will take better care of myself.
- I will not play the victim!
- When I need breaks and vacations, I will take them and come back to school recharged, refreshed, and ready to go to the next level.
- My students will not be negative statistics.
- I will hire the right staff to work with my students.

Find a few positive affirmations that work for you and write them down. Repeat them every morning before you walk into your building or classroom. Say them in the middle of the day and at the end of the day. Say them often. They will be the constant reminder that you matter to your students and staff. These young men are like sponges and will absorb what you teach them if you are fair and they can see that you are committed to helping them achieve.

Conclusion

Our student population has changed. Whether you are a white educator or an educator who identifies with a particular race or ethnicity, it's important that you show your students—all your students—that you care about them. We must educate, activate, and motivate all students at all times. Know that your Black and Latino male students are capable of learning and being great, of being success stories. Don't take students' actions personally. If you continually work on your responses and build trust, you will be highly effective at what you do.

Many educators burn out easily (secondary traumatic stress and compassion fatigue is very prevalent among educators), so self-help is extremely important. Finding a balance in your life and filling your life with activities not related to teaching is essential to your being able function as an effective teacher or administrator.

CHAPTER 4

Building Strong Relationships with Your Students and Staff

Relationship-building is key to improving how educators relate to and reach students—especially Black and Latino male students. The lack of positive interaction among teachers, administrators, parents, and students is one of the reasons we lose too many of our students. You cannot teach those you can't reach. Whether you have been doing this work for one year or 31 years, the fact is that students respond better to and respect those who build relationships with them. It's tough for students to communicate with someone they don't have a good relationship with. The educator who builds strong relationships with students will be the most successful.

Strong, healthy relationships share the following characteristics:

- Mutual respect
- Trust
- Honesty
- Cooperation
- Allowance for individuality
- Good communication
- Anger control
- Fair disagreements
- Problem solving
- Celebration of self-confidence
- Modeling

Trust

Trust your students and give them the benefit of the doubt.
Trust will require that you be honest with your students as
well as with yourself. You must work through the points of
view of your students who are often hurt and easily offended
and find a middle ground where you and your students can
function comfortably. Don't expect students to conform in
ways that limit their creativity and ability to express themselves positively. Give students room to be individuals.
Communicate with students, including working through
misunderstandings, as you would have them communicate
with you. Allow students to work through their feelings about
something that is unsettling—and allow yourself to do the
same—even if it means a few extra minutes of discussion after
school or after class. Even when you feel like the young man
is not listening, love out of him what's inside. Look past the
stubborn behavior. Students will eventually respond in a positive way to someone they feel they can trust.

Respect

Most people have different scales by which to weigh respect
… and disrespect. What is your definition of respect? What
is your definition of disrespect? How do you gauge what's
respectful versus what is disrespectful with your students and
staff? Most school districts don't have any guidelines by which
to determine discipline techniques. Educators determine what
is respectful or disrespectful based on their own definitions,
perceptions, and biases.

I have walked into school buildings and classrooms nationally and witnessed numerous examples of disrespect from both students and educators. *Yes, I have witnessed school leaders, teachers, and counselors being disrespectful to students.* We are supposed to set the example of what leadership looks like. We can't do that when we lead with our emotions.

Disrespect

Disrespect is taught just like respect is taught. Regardless of how you grew up or what you grew up with or without, disrespect is disrespect.

Yelling at students and showing anger shows that you have taken students' actions personally and causes students to dislike you. Attitude is everything. If students are constantly offended by you, your actions, and your words, they will not value your expertise, your opinion, or your leadership, and it will be hard to reach and teach them. Administrators, define disrespect, including examples that will not be tolerated, so it's clear for all staff members and students. Sometimes rules need to be tweaked. Sometimes an apology is in order. Sometimes students and staff just need to be heard.

Practice What You Preach

As administrators and teachers, you set the example and tone for your classroom and building. If you correct students, staff, and parents about the way they dress, make sure you are dressing professionally and appropriately—not like you are heading out to the nightclub or lounge. If there is a "no cell phones" rule, you shouldn't be on your cell phone checking your Instagram, Facebook, Snapchat, and Twitter accounts during school hours. If there is a "no cursing" rule, you shouldn't be using curse words with or around your students. The rules that apply to students should apply to you as well. Following the same rules as your students builds camaraderie and healthy relationships with Black and Latino male students.

All, Not Some

Educators must be committed, dedicated, and consistent in the right way every single day. Treat all students like successes despite their background. Treat the students with the worst grades as you treat those with the best grades. All students—including the ones who misbehave and the ones who have a problem with structure—are reachable when the right educator is involved.

Get to Know and Stay Informed About Your Students

Each of your Black and Latino male students will be different in the way they receive and process information. They will bring into your classroom a wide variety of home-life experiences that will influence the way they present themselves on a daily basis. Get to know the different economic statuses of students so that you can understand them. The more you understand each student's needs, shortcomings, strengths, and motivating factors, the easier it will be to get them involved in the learning process.

Ask Probing Questions

One way to better inform yourself about your students is to ask probing questions. Early in the school year, have students form a circle, introduce yourself to the class, and then have students introduce themselves and share one thing that they like to do. (Administrators, do the same in a staff meeting or in professional development workshop with staff.) Ask about their favorite subjects in school, extracurricular activities, and siblings, and find out whether they are the oldest, youngest, or middle children and what they plan to do during school breaks. Customize the list of questions for your students. Don't attempt to get too personal. Just stick to the kinds of questions that will allow you to get a better read of what influences them daily.

Unless you know their close friends and family members, it is nearly impossible to know anything about or get to know your Black and Latino male students without asking them questions. Watching the news and allowing mental models and stereotypes to dictate your thoughts about your students who may resemble criminals on television is not a way to get to know them. You will learn a lot from kids just by asking the right questions and talking to them. Begin the school year with an introduction that includes an account of you or someone close to you overcoming an obstacle. Provide specific details, such as setbacks encountered, mental blocks, and what it took to overcome the obstacle. This is an effective way to allow your students to see your human side. If you share details about yourself and gently probe, most will share information about their own obstacles, and over time, you will find out who is homeless, hungry, abused, or neglected.

"Get to Know Your Neighbor" Fridays

Over time, you will also discover whose parents are incarcerated or divorced.

When I taught at Arlington High School in Indianapolis, Indiana, we would have "get to know your neighbor" Fridays. At that time, students would answer a series of questions about themselves and what was important to them. One Friday, the question was, "Are both your parents still together, married, divorced, separated, never married, and what are your thoughts about it?" Students gave a range of answers, and elaboration was encouraged but not forced. The more students elaborated, the more I was able to understand them. One of my students got very emotional when speaking about the absence of his father and how it affected his everyday life. I was used to this student joking around all the time, and then I understood why: he was hiding a lot of pain. As a result of our Friday conversations, I was able to refer him to the help he needed to start the healing process.

Verbal Exchanges

Verbal exchanges aren't always productive, especially in the beginning. Verbal exchanges always worked really well for me and my students. If verbal exchanges don't work for you, feel free to do a written exercise that doesn't require students to write their names at the top of the paper.

A Sample Exercise

The following is an exercise that you can do with your students that involves no lesson plans. It is strictly to get to know them and allow them to get to know you. This exercise should be done verbally initially (and if that doesn't work, make it a written exercise). Make sure you participate as well.

Ask questions such as

- What makes school fun for you?
- What are your likes and dislikes?
- What problems have you encountered in the past?
- What problems are you currently dealing with?
- What are your expectations of your teacher?
- What are your expectations of your principal?
- Is there anything hindering you from being successful?
- How can I help you address any obstacles to your success?
- What are your extracurricular activities or pastimes outside school?
- What are your future goals (e.g., graduate from high school, attend college, join the military, get a job, become an entrepreneur)?
- What do you like or dislike about school?
- What mistakes have you made with your teachers or administrators in the past?
- What is something teachers or administrators do that drives you crazy?
- What is something you have done with a group of people that you wouldn't have done alone?
- What is one thing about your home situation you wish you could change?
- Do you know someone who has been murdered? Talk (or write) about it.
- Do you know someone who has been incarcerated? Who? How has it affected you?
- What is one thing that you need to work on?
- What is your greatest strength?
- What are your weaknesses?

Ask these questions early and often to begin the process of relationship-building. Depending on your approach, some students may tell all on day one. While some Black and Latino male students feel like they know within a few minutes whether or not they can trust you, it will take others longer to open up because they have been lied to and hurt in the past so much that it's hard for them to trust anyone—so be patient with them. Just because a student doesn't tell all on day one doesn't mean he won't eventually.

Listen to Students

The six essential rules of good listening are

- Be silent when others are speaking.
- Ask good questions to get the conversation going.
- Think before responding.
- Avoid outside distractions (phone, television, laptop, etc.).
- Show you are interested through your positive body language.
- Control the tone of your voice.

Contemporary Slang

Listening to students—not just what they say but the way that they say it—helps us stay current with contemporary slang. Students communicate differently today than when we were kids. Social media and texting has led to whole new categories of words and phrases. When I hear students use words I don't know or in an unfamiliar context, I simply ask them to explain what they're saying. Unless they are afraid of getting punished, they are generally happy to fill me in.

Here's a selection of slang terms that I have heard used among Black and Latino male students:

- *Rachet*: Nasty. An insulting and demeaning term.
- *THOT*: "That hoe over there." A disrespectful way of referring to females.
- *Out of my body:* High or drunk.
- *Thirsty*: Desperate for sex or wants to be with multiple people.
- *Basic*: Boring and average. It's another insulting term.
- *On fleek*: Something is on point (that is, a way of complimenting someone).
- *Stiff*: Physically strong.
- *Getting lit*: Drinking, smoking, partying, and the like.
- *Turn up*: Get your energy up, get excited about something. It means the same as "lit." It can also mean getting "live" (e.g., excited or worked up) at a party or gathering.
- *Dope*: Fun and exciting.
- *Fried*: Funny.
- *Cap or capping*: Overdoing something.

Educators, when you hear certain words you don't know or understand, don't be afraid to ask the meaning of those words. Keep a journal or ledger with a running list of those words and review the list from time to time. (As some of these words are inappropriate or unsuitable in most settings, please don't begin using them with your students.)

Know What Motivates Your Students

Find out what motivates students outside school and bring it into the classroom if you possibly can. If a certain percentage of students scores well on a test, provide them with snacks. Create a class Facebook page and post how well students are doing.

Tangible Evidence of Future Options

I have invited doctors, lawyers, construction workers, professional athletes, entrepreneurs, and the like to speak to my students so that they could be motivated by seeing tangible evidence of future options. You would be surprised how easy it was to get these individuals to come in to speak to my class. I met most of them at social events, and I just simply asked. I explained the importance of giving back to our kids and how they could make a difference. I would target organizations that were supposed to be giving back to their respective communities and hold them accountable. In turn, my students were exposed to individuals they wouldn't have otherwise been exposed to.

Music

Music is another great tool I have used to keep students motivated and engaged. The right music can change the mood and climate of a classroom. I would play the music they liked when the majority did well on tests, and it motivated them to want to do better every time. It became contagious. Students were encouraging each other in lessons just so they could be rewarded later with the music they liked. Some of my students even shared their own music that they had made or were working on at the time. Music motivated my students to strive for excellence.

Monitoring

It's up to you to find out what motivates your students. A basic start can be taking a written or verbal poll of what they like and dislike. This makes it easier to provide these types of activities and events. It only takes a few minutes. As the year goes on, monitor your students' progress and keep a record of what keeps them constantly motivated. Is it a certain kind of activity, topic, or the way you present materials? Is it working in groups or alone? The more you know about how your students enjoy learning best, the better able you'll be to keep them engaged and motivated.

Give Your Black and Latino Male Students Leadership Roles

The only way to teach leadership is to model it and practice it with your students. Just because a student has high self-esteem doesn't mean he is a good leader. Just because a student doesn't say much doesn't mean he can't become an effective leader. Leadership requires trust, loyalty, consistency, perseverance, compassion, and resolve. Benefits include confidence, growth, better productivity, and fewer distractions and behavior issues. If you build trust, you will receive better buy-in from your students.

Following is a list of leadership roles to consider for your Black and Latino male students:

- Taking attendance
- Passing out papers, tests, and so on
- Running errands
- Tutoring students in need
- Mentoring other students
- Making copies
- Making announcements

- Passing out snacks
- Making phone calls
- Answering the phone
- (Administrators), crafting e-mails to send out to the student body

Be Transparent/Tell the Truth

Be transparent about your hurts and disappointments. Tell the truth about wanting to quit at times but not giving up. Tell the truth about having grown up socially and economically disadvantaged but refusing to use those things as excuses. Tell the truth about your upbringing, whether it was ideal or troubled. Tell the truth about trauma—including abuse, neglect, or abandonment—because someone may benefit from your story. Be transparent about the consequences of bad relationships that you have been in and learned from. Talk about the consequences of choosing the wrong friends. Let students know that if they show you their friends, you will show them their future. Let them know that even though you're an educator, you have family members who chose another route—a less desirable one.

If you are a male teacher, tell the truth if you have disrespected women in the past and how you have learned from your mistakes. If you are a female teacher, be frank about the harm disrespect from males has caused you. Our young men must be taught to respect one another, themselves, and females. Let your students know that their lived experiences are valid and valued by you. Who they are, what they know, and what they live daily is important. Whether a student is privileged or has a heart-wrenching story is a factor in terms of how they respond to the educational setting.

Being transparent and honest allows time for positive relationships to be built. Your transparency also has the potential to encourage students to navigate through the school system, especially when your story entails overcoming obstacles while getting your education.

Lives Are at Stake

We have to be more than teachers and administrators. We have to be mentors. We have to be coaches. We have to be leaders. Your transparency can save a life. Your transparency can help eliminate some anxiety and stress in students. It is not always comfortable to be transparent because doing so means you are exposing your personal shortcomings and struggles, and that is not easy. While you don't want to reveal intimate details, when there is a pertinent subject that surfaces and you have something to contribute that will help that student, share it.

Correcting Behavior

I've told my students that I got into fights, was suspended from school and kicked off the bus, had trouble reading, was too shy to talk to girls, fought through anger and anxiety issues, never met my father, and that I hung with drug dealers growing up. I've told them that I made too many mistakes to count. It's not about the number of mistakes you have made; it's about correcting the behavior. When students make mistakes, remind them not to dwell on them and to focus on what they learned from them and on how to correct them.

Healing

Transparency is also a way of healing for educators. Many of us have not been honest with ourselves about who we really are. Some of us aren't honest with our loved ones or our students. Some educators are hiding their hurts and shortcomings. Many of us continue to carry around or hide pain that we should have let go of a long time ago.

Admit Mistakes

If you have been in this profession for any amount of time, you will have made your share of mistakes. The question is, what do you do after you make a mistake? How do you handle it? The answer to this question is—or should be—very simple. Be blatantly honest with your students. If you do that, they will respect you for it.

———

I remember being excited about teaching a lesson only to be told by a former student that I'd taught it incorrectly. When I asked the student why he hadn't told me earlier, he replied, "You were so excited about teaching it that I didn't want to mess up your flow." Although we both chuckled about it, I knew what I needed to do next. The next day, I got up in front of my class, explained that I had taught the lesson incorrectly, and apologized.

By admitting my mistake and apologizing for it, I gained the respect of my students. After that, I noticed that students apologized to each other more when they made mistakes or disrespected each other.

Kids learn by example. They watch *everything*. This is one of the main reasons I watch what I say and how I say it, how I dress, how I conduct myself, how I handle conflict, and so on. If you do happen to make a mistake with your students, apologize for it immediately. Some may laugh or poke fun at you at first, but they will respect you for it, which is most important. No one is perfect. Educators lose opportunities for their students to see their human side when they walk around acting as though they don't make mistakes.

After apologizing, I acknowledged in front of the class the student who brought my mistake to my attention. When I noticed that he began to tear up, I changed the subject. After class, he told me no one had ever acknowledged him before and that he was grateful. Recognizing him allowed us to begin to build a bond. But more importantly, he felt empowered as a result. I watched his confidence begin to manifest; it made me feel good to witness this.

Never Show Anger

A person who shows anger is a person who has lost control of the situation and is taking someone's words or actions personally. We must never take the actions of our students personally. Kids are in pain daily. Even when students provoke us intentionally, we must make every effort to understand that the student's aggression is more than likely misplaced. The root of their anger more than likely has nothing to do with us.

The four factors that cause anger are

- Fear
- Frustration
- Pain
- Hurt

If you are angry about something, I can guarantee one of those four factors is the culprit. Anger plus anger equals … more anger. Hurt people hurt people. Showing anger can also cause students to dislike you. You may think, "I'm not here for them to like me." Maybe not, but you may want to consider evaluating yourself and your approach anyway. Such a stance about your relationship with your students may be the very thing preventing you from really being effective. Whatever the case may be, showing anger to an angry student is a bad idea and will only result in a missed opportunity for improvement for you and the student.

What Can Happen

Back in the mid-1990s, I helped coach student athletes. The head coach was very abrasive with everyone to the point where nobody wanted to be around him. When he would take time off to go on fishing trips, the coach would turn the team over to me and I would immediately take the opportunity to build strong relationships with the team. Although I set high expectations, the atmosphere was no longer tense, and we enjoyed winning our competitions without the yelling and screaming.

When the head coach would return from his trips, the atmosphere suddenly became toxic. Players withdrew in the face of his abrasiveness (as it reminded them too much of their lives at home and their neighborhoods). After one trip, the head coach noticed that the students became glum when he was around and called a team meeting. "This is my team! I run the show here!" he yelled. I thought to myself that it was easy for him to say that after he'd gone fishing when the team needed him most, when the team was successful in his absence. The athletes expressed their concerns and many of them wanted to quit as a result of their interactions with him.

That coach never regained the respect of all of his athletes, even though many of them needed his guidance. Winning championships doesn't matter when kids are hurt in the process. Students don't respond well if you spend your time yelling at them when they need a positive voice. The sad part about the whole situation is that he refused to change. He was stuck in his ways and didn't seem to care who didn't like it. Instead of meeting these student athletes where they were, he labeled them as "quitters" and said to me, "Let them quit!"

Don't Make Matters Worse

Not showing anger means remaining calm when students lash out. Allow students who are angry or upset the opportunity to work out their feelings in a safe environment where they won't be judged. When they are comfortable, they will come back to communicate verbally. Yelling and screaming at kids never solves any issues. It doesn't help the situation at all. In fact, it makes matters worse. Remember how you felt when someone yelled and screamed at you. It is detrimental, especially to Black and Latino males who are most likely already in pain about something. Teach these students to use their words to express how they feel so they can process it and move on. The pain and anger built up in some of these young men didn't appear overnight and neither will earning and winning their trust. Instead of asking, "Why are you so angry?", ask questions like, "What are you in pain about?", "How can I help?",

"What is causing you so much stress?", and, "Can you tell me why you are so frustrated?"

Provide Honest and Positive Feedback

If you want to get the best out of students, you must set high expectations for them and provide them with positive reinforcement when they fall short. When it feels like society and the world is tearing you down daily, a positive word goes a long way. When you provide positive, constructive feedback, students walk away feeling good about improving their behaviors.

Start with a Positive, End with a Positive, and Ask Questions

What you begin with and end with is extremely important. When giving feedback, always start with a positive and end with a positive. Talk about the negatives and things that need improvement in the middle. For example, if a young man is not doing well in math class, instead of telling him in front of everyone that he is bad at math, try asking him, "How do you think you're doing?", "What have been your biggest struggles in math?", or "What kind of help do you need?" I would say, "You are struggling a little, but this is fixable. Let's work on a plan together to get you the support you need."

Get to the Root of the Problem

At the end of the day, we want these young men to be successful in and out of the classroom, and it starts with getting to the root of the problem. If it's a behavior problem, say something like, "Tell me what your thought process was when you made that decision" or ask, "What would you do if you were in my situation and a student did what you just did?" Approaching the problem in this way is extremely important and can make or break a situation. Aim to make the conversation nonthreatening.

Delivering Feedback

When delivering feedback, consider the following (Reynolds, 2013):

- Be sensitive to the individual needs of students.
- Give feedback to keep students "on target" for achievement.
- Student feedback can be given verbally, nonverbally, or in written form.
- Give genuine praise.
- Invite students to give *you* feedback.

Have Students Evaluate Your Teaching

My evaluation process as a teacher always included my students. I wanted to know how they viewed me. So many times, we view ourselves differently than our students view us. I wanted to know how effectively I was doing my job, so I developed a survey that my students could complete anonymously if they so chose.

Some of the questions included on the survey were

- What is your overall level of comfort in this classroom on a scale of one to 10 (with 10 being the most comfortable)?
- Would you recommend this class to your classmates? If no, why not?

- What is one thing you like about this class? Why?
- What is one thing you dislike about this class? Why?
- What can I do to improve this class for you and your classmates?
- What is something that you feel you need to improve on to make your experience in this class better?
- What is something I do that you don't like? Why?
- What is something you would like to share with me that I may not know about you?

My students were always very honest with me, and the last question allowed me to learn more about my students. I found out that many of them looked at me as more than their teacher. I meant much more to them than I knew. This survey revealed a lot of hidden hurts experienced by my students. I appreciated their honesty. Ninety percent were dealing with some type of trauma—from neglect to domestic violence to financial issues to addiction to sexual abuse. It's amazing how much you can find out during a survey from your students. It's important to ask them questions and probe. I remember the hardships that one student shared: he wasn't eating properly every day (most days they didn't have food to eat) and his father chose drugs and alcohol over him, his mother, and his siblings and abandoned the family.

As to my own performance, most students mentioned that I was fair and consistent. For example, I was late one day by two minutes and had to do 25 push-ups (per the rule we came up with together when someone was late). They appreciated that I followed the rule—while in slacks and a shirt and tie. I didn't receive a perfect report. Two students said they thought I was abrasive and mean at times. One student said that I showed favoritism to my students who were athletes or other students that I liked. Instead of getting defensive, I took a hard look at what I thought I was doing wrong and made some adjustments. I also thanked them for their honesty and let them know that honest feedback is extremely important. I knew what I needed to do to adjust and improve.

Capture the Heart

To educate the mind, you must first capture the heart. Have students complete a survey to capture their hearts. Don't take it personally if someone tells you something that you need to improve on or mentions something to you that they may not like. Embrace it as a new opportunity to get better. Our goal is to reach all these young men, and capturing their hearts is part of that.

Promote Resilience

Teach students to bounce back from trauma and adversity. Students need to know that a setback is not the end of the story; it's a setup for a comeback. It makes a difference in their classroom performance when they learn to be resilient in every aspect of life and to bounce back from adversity. This will require some to step outside their comfort zones. Share with your students your failures and disappointments and how you overcame them. Be honest about whether you are still fighting to overcome them or have learned to live with them. Be empathetic about the plight of your students, but don't feel sorry for them. Spend time teaching them how to overcome obstacles.

Teaching students to be resilient is necessary to building stronger bonds. It helps them push past hurtful thoughts in order to be more focused on school. To promote resilience in students

- Teach students that they can change the narrative if they choose to.
- Let them know their current situation is not their destination.
- Encourage them to learn how to cope with difficult people.
- Remind them that how they respond to a situation is totally up to them.
- Let them know that hard work always pays off in the long run.
- Teach them how to control their emotions.
- Encourage them to seek counseling for traumas they have experienced.

Speak to Your Students' Spirits

It's important that our students hear something positive about themselves every day. Not every now and then. Not when you feel like it. Every day.

Write down four things you plan to say to your students and staff on a daily basis. In case you can't think of any, here are a few examples:

- You matter to me!
- You are somebody!
- You will be successful!
- You are smart!
- I believe in you!
- Today is going to be a great day!
- Never give up!
- You can do all things!
- Today is a new day with new possibilities!

Many Black and Latino young men are daily bombarded with negative words and suggestions. The conversations that they have with their peers is often negative. Profanity is the norm because many of them learned to talk this way from other family members. Since negativity is the norm for some of these young men, don't be surprised if it takes a while for some to adjust to positivity. The first few encounters may be shocking to them. Don't be surprised if you get some resistance. Resistance doesn't mean failure on your part; it means that the relationship is still developing. Even when the relationship becomes strong, some may revert to old behaviors and resist.

Something Simple

Sometimes a simple "thank you" goes a long way. A smile goes a long way. Thank your students and staff for their efforts often. Keep speaking those positive words every day. Even when you don't feel like it. You may be the only person who speaks positively to a student. Convincing students that they can do well in your class and successfully complete high school all starts with your words.

Choose Your Words Carefully

Be thoughtful in your choice of words. Many students have trigger words that cause them to become upset. These particular students have been consistent targets for negative words. Words hurt people. Hurt people hurt people. We must also choose our words wisely when speaking with our students. We must speak to our students where we want them to go. If you want them to be successful, speak to them like they are successful. We must speak to Black and Latino males in ways that they may not be used to—professionally, structured, and uplifting. Doing so will get their attention, and they will know from the beginning what the expectation is in your classroom or building. Ensure that your words are building students and staff up and not tearing them down.

Self-Help For Educators and Administrators

No one is going to take care of you better than ... you. Balance your life. Learn how to leave work at work, which may be tough if your norm is to take work life home. School can be very stressful, and your significant other, children, and pets shouldn't have to relive your experiences.

Stress

The definition of stress is a state of mental or emotional strain or tension resulting from adverse or very demanding circumstances. We all have experienced stress at some point in our lives. It is totally up to us how we decide to deal with that stress. Stressors include

- Money management/finances
- House cleaning/clutter
- School preparation/getting kids ready for school
- Homework
- Bedtime routines
- Making healthy meal choices

It's tough being an educator and finding the balance between home and education. So many demands are put on you. Signs of stress include temper, chronic fatigue, cynicism, headaches, migraines, hypertension, heart disease, forgetfulness, and secondary traumatic stress (STS). Many educators suffer from STS, the symptoms of which include compassion fatigue, withdrawal, irritability, anger, feeling overwhelmed, inability to sleep, feelings of isolation, and consistently worrying about students and their health issues. STS will not go away if you don't change your lifestyle and thought processes.

Loss

We work with students every day, and losing a student is very stressful.

On a Friday I was speaking to one of my students who was doing very well in my class about the importance of education and the next day he was stabbed to death at a party. Six days later I attended his funeral.

It broke my heart. He was more than a good kid. He was going places. I spent several months trying to cope with his death. What I didn't realize was that I was losing the rest of my class because I was stuck on this one student who was no longer there. I wasn't being fair to the students who were there—and hurting as much as I was.

On our first day back at school after the funeral, we were numb and silent. I came to my senses and reminded the students that we must push forward. I told them that we would never forget the young man but that we had to keep moving forward.

Solutions to Stress

- *Don't try to remember everything.* If you forget something, don't be hard on yourself. Use a note book or tablet to keep track of what you need to remember.
- *Stop trying to please everyone.* No matter how hard you try, someone is going to be upset with you. Do more to please yourself than to please others.
- *Take care of your mind and body.*
  —*Exercise.* Find a routine with consistency
  —*Eat right.* Find a balance in your eating to stay healthy
  —*Meditate.* Quiet time is essential for your soul
  —*Get rest.* This job is tough. Don't overdo it. Get plenty of rest.
  —*Cut people off.* Cut off anyone who's causing you stress as opposed to helping you deal with your stress.

- *Avoid starting your day with false energy.* Replace coffee/caffeine with healthy juice, wheat grass, water, affirmations, positive thoughts and words, meditation and joy, and peace and centering.
- *Talk to your problems rather than talking about your problems.* Speak out against the problems in your life. Take steps to correct them rather than talk about them.

Also, carve out time for yourself that includes you and only you. For example

- Go to the gym.
- Get your nails done.
- Take time to cry and laugh.
- Find a balance between home and work.

- Take a break from your children.
- Protect your peace.
- Take a vacation.
- Control your emotions.

Conclusion

Although building strong relationships with students and staff is challenging, it's not impossible. Once students know you care, they slowly drop their guard. For these young men, it may take some time, but it's not out of the question.

There is a difference between being respectful and being disrespectful. As educators, we must control our emotions and gauge our responses no matter the outlandish statements or actions by students.

What words will you speak over your students and staff—and yourself— daily?

Self-care is extremely important for all educators. We can all do a better job of taking care of ourselves. No one will care for you like you care for yourself.

FINAL THOUGHTS

Thanks for being in education. As an educator, you are special. What you do daily impacts our society. If you do it right (not perfectly), your impact can be felt for generations to come. There is great fulfillment when you touch the lives of others. If you have already experienced it for yourself, you are moving in the right direction.

I have been in education for nearly 25 years. I didn't know when I started all those years ago the impact that I would have on my students and the fulfillment that teaching these students would bring. When I'm in a grocery store, on a plane, or at an event and I hear someone say, "Mr. Jackson" or "Coach Jackson," I beam with pride because I know it is one of my former students or someone whose life I changed during my time as an educator.

I hear countless affirming and thoughtful words that motivate me to continue my mission of educating others. I weekly receive messages on social media from students asking me for advice, or whether I remember them, or simply letting me know that they are doing well or thanking me. It's surreal, especially when I'm told about something positive I did that I'd forgotten about or when I hear about some that I'd given very little weight, such as a simple word of encouragement.

If you haven't experienced students coming back to see you or reaching out to you via social media, put the time, effort, and patience into the task of thoughtfully educating *all* your students and just wait. The joy and excitement you will feel when you see the fruits of your labor in the guise of former students grown up with families and flourishing in the roles as fathers, husbands, and productive citizens. It's sometimes breathtaking. It is in those moments that it all comes full circle, and you will see with your own eyes that your efforts toward those distant and seemingly unreachable young men were well worth your time.

So, when you walk into your classroom or building and are faced with Black and Latino male students, you have an opportunity to put all that you have learned to work. What choices will you make? When your students come back in five, 10, or 15 years, what will they say to you? What impact will you have had on them?

Be the educator you were called to be. Be the educator you wanted and needed as a student. Make every effort to find fulfillment in this calling for yourself as well as for your Black and Latino male students. Be the educator they need.

REFERENCES

American Psychological Association. (2006). Stereotype threat widens achievement gap. Retrieved from https://www.apa.org/research/action/stereotype

Anne E. Casey Foundation. Kids Count Data Center. Children in poverty by race and ethnicity in the United States. Retrieved from https://datacenter.kidscount.org/data/tables/44-children-in-poverty-by-race-and-ethnicity.

Centers for Disease Control and Prevention. (2018a). Leading causes of death (LCOD) by age group, Black males-United States, 2015. Retrieved from https://www.cdc.gov/healthequity/lcod/men/2015/black/index.htm

Centers for Disease Control and Prevention. (2018b). Leading causes of death (LCOD) by age group, Hispanic males-United States, 2015. Retrieved from https://www.cdc.gov/healthequity/lcod/men/2015/hispanic/index.htm

Cohen, M. (2015, April 28). How for-profit prisons have become the biggest lobby no one is talking about. Washington Post. Retrieved from https://www.washingtonpost.com/posteverything/wp/2015/04/28/how-for-profit-prisons-have-become-the-biggest-lobby-no-one-is-talking-about/?utm_term=.5938b2032526

Harriot, M. (2017, October 3). Why we never talk about black-on-black crime. The Root. Retrieved from https://www.theroot.com/why-we-never-talk-about-black-on-black-crime-an-answer-1819092337

National Center for Education Statistics. (2018). English language learners in public schools. Retrieved from https://nces.ed.gov /programs/coe/indicator_cgf.asp

National Gang Center. (2018). National youth gang survey analysis. Informed. *Retrieved.* from http://www.nationalgangcenter.gov /Survey-Analysis.

Patterson, O. (2015). *The cultural matrix: Understanding black youth.* Cambridge, MA: Harvard University Press.

Reynolds, L. (2013, June 11). Giving students feedback: 20 tips to do it right. Retrieved from https://www.opencolleges.edu.au/informed /features/giving-student-feedback/

The Sentencing Project. (2017). Criminal justice facts. Retrieved from https://www.sentencingproject.org/criminal-justice-facts/

Stanford Open Policing Project. (2018). Findings. Retrieved from https://openpolicing.stanford.edu/findings/

Williams, M. (2011). Colorblind ideology is a form of racism. Psychology Today. Retrieved from https://www.psychologytoday.com/us/ blog /culturally-speaking/201112/colorblind-ideology-is-form-racism

INDEX

ABOUT THE AUTHOR

Robert Jackson began his teaching career with a no-nonsense but caring approach to education in Indianapolis public schools more than 20 years ago—after being cut from the NFL (Minnesota Vikings). Wanting to make a bigger impact in education he created a No More Excuses curriculum—which has been featured in publications nationally and is being used in K–12 schools, colleges, and universities in the United States and Canada.

Jackson, one of the most sought-after experts on teaching cultural diversity, restorative practices, socioemotional learning, working with students who have experienced trauma, and how to educate Black and Latino males in the country, received his Bachelor's of Science degree in industrial technology from Western Kentucky University. He has delivered numerous keynote addresses and continually holds workshops for educators, administrators, parents, and students.

The author of five books—*Black Men Stand Up, A Boys Guide to Manhood, A Young Woman's Guide to Womanhood, Put a Stop to Bullying*, and *Solutions to Educating Black and Latino Males*—Jackson has written articles for ASCD's *Educational Leadership*. He has spoken at the national conferences of many professional organizations, including ASCD, SDE, CAAASA, NABSE, SREB, School Discipline, and ESEA National Title One.

Jackson is a member of Kappa Alpha Psi Fraternity, Inc. and the NFL Players Association. He can be reached at robert@robertjacksonmotivates.com, via his website www.robertjacksonmotivates.com, and you can follow him on Twitter @RJMotivates, on Instagram @robjmotivates, and on Facebook on the Robert Jackson Motivates fan page.

Related ASCD Resources

At the time of publication, the following resources were available (ASCD stock numbers appear in parentheses):

Print Products

Motivating Black Males to Achieve in School & In Life by Baruti K. Kafele (#109013)

Closing the Attitude Gap: How to Fire Up Your Students to Strive for Success by Baruti K. Kafele (#114006)

Keeping It Real and Relevant: Building Authentic Relations in Your Diverse Classroom by Igancio Lopez (#117049)

Raising Black Students' Achievement Through Culturally Responsive Teaching by Johnnie McKinley (#110004)

Educating Everybody's Children: Diverse Teaching Strategies for Diverse Learners, Revised and Expanded 2nd Edition by Robert W. Cole (#107003)

The Motivated Brain: Improving Student Attention, Engagement, and Perseverance by Gayle Gregory & Martha Kaufeldt (#115041)

Discipline with Dignity: How to Build Responsibility, Relationships, and Respect in Your Classroom by Richard L. Curwin, Allen N. Mendler, and Brian D. Mendler (#118018)

Turning High-Poverty Schools Into High-Performing Schools by William H. Parrett and Kathleen M. Budge (#109003)

Qualities of Effective Teachers, 3rd Edition, by James H. Stronge (#118042)

Meeting Students Where They Live: Motivation in Urban Schools by Richard L. Curwin (#109110)

Learning to Choose, Choosing to Learn: The Key to Student Motivation and Achievement by Mike Anderson (#116015)

How to Motivate Reluctant Learners (Mastering the Principles of Great Teaching series) by Robyn R. Jackson (#110076)

Teachers as Classroom Coaches: How to Motivate Students Across the Content Areas by Andi Stix and Frank Hrbek (#106031)

Activating the Desire to Learn by Bob Sullo (#107009)

Learning in the Fast Lane: 8 Ways to Put All Students on the Road to Academic Success by Suzy Pepper Rollins (#114026)

Minding the Achievement Gap One Classroom at a Time by Jane E. Pollock, Sharon M. Ford, and Margaret M. Black (#112005)

Teaching With Poverty in Mind: What Being Poor Does to Kids' Brains and What Schools Can Do About It by Eric Jensen (#109074)

For up-to-date information about ASCD resources, go to www.ascd.org. You can search the complete archives of *Educational Leadership* at www.ascd.org/el.

ASCD myTeachSource®

Download resources from a professional learning platform with hundreds of research-based best practices and tools for your classroom at http://myteachsource.ascd.org/.

For more information, send an e-mail to member@ascd.org; call 1-800-933-2723 or 703-578-9600; send a fax to 703-575-5400; or write to Information Services, ASCD, 1703 N. Beauregard St., Alexandria, VA 22311-1714 USA.

 ascd whole child

The ASCD Whole Child approach is an effort to transition from a focus on narrowly defined academic achievement to one that promotes the long-term development and success of all children. Through this approach, ASCD supports educators, families, community members, and policymakers as they move from a vision about educating the whole child to sustainable, collaborative actions.

Becoming the Educator They Need relates to **all five** tenets.

For more about the ASCD Whole Child approach, visit **www.ascd.org/wholechild.**

WHOLE CHILD
TENETS

1 HEALTHY
Each student enters school healthy and learns about and practices a healthy lifestyle.

2 SAFE
Each student learns in an environment that is physically and emotionally safe for students and adults.

3 ENGAGED
Each student is actively engaged in learning and is connected to the school and broader community.

4 SUPPORTED
Each student has access to personalized learning and is supported by qualified, caring adults.

5 CHALLENGED
Each student is challenged academically and prepared for success in college or further study and for employment and participation in a global environment.